Bloom's BioCritiques:

Fyodor Dostoevsky

Bloom's BioCritiques

Dante Alighieri
Maya Angelou
Jane Austen
Jorge Luis Borges
The Brontë Sisters
Gwendolyn Brooks
Lord Byron
Miguel de Cervantes
Geoffrey Chaucer
Anton Chekhov
Joseph Conrad
Stephen Crane
Charles Dickens
Emily Dickinson
Fyodor Dostoevsky
William Faulkner
F. Scott Fitzgerald
Robert Frost
Ernest Hemingway
Langston Hughes
Zora Neale Hurston
Franz Kafka
Stephen King
Arthur Miller
John Milton
Toni Morrison
Edgar Allan Poe
J.D. Salinger
William Shakespeare
John Steinbeck
Henry David Thoreau
Mark Twain
Alice Walker
Eudora Welty
Walt Whitman
Tennessee Williams
Virginia Woolf

Bloom's BioCritiques

FYODOR DOSTOEVSKY

Edited and with an introduction by
Harold Bloom
Sterling Professor of the Humanities
Yale University

CHELSEA HOUSE
PUBLISHERS
A Haights Cross Communications ✦ Company
Philadelphia

Library of Congress Cataloging-in-Publication Data

Fyodor Dostoevsky / Harold Bloom, editor.
      p. cm. — (Bloom's biocritiques)
  Includes bibliographical references and index.
  ISBN 0-7910-8117-6 (alk. paper)
  1. Dostoyevsky, Fyodor, 1821–1881—Criticism and interpretation. I. Bloom,
Harold. II. Series.
  PG3328.Z6F963 2004
  891.73'3—dc22
                                        2004013049

Chelsea House Publishers
2080 Cabot Boulevard West, Suite 201
Langhorne, PA 19047

http://www.chelseahouse.com

Contributing editor: Rachel Thomas
Cover design by Keith Trego
Cover: © Bettman/CORBIS
Layout by EJB Publishing Services

CONTENTS

USER'S GUIDE

These volumes are designed to introduce the reader to the life and work of the world's literary masters. Each volume begins with Harold Bloom's essay "The Work in the Writer" and a volume-specific introduction also written by Professor Bloom. Following these unique introductions is an engaging biography that discusses the major life events and important literary accomplishments of the author under consideration.

Furthermore, each volume includes an original critique that not only traces the themes, symbols, and ideas apparent in the author's works, but strives to put those works into a cultural and historical perspective. In addition to the original critique is a brief selection of significant critical essays previously published on the author and his or her works followed by a concise and informative chronology of the writer's life. Finally, each volume concludes with a bibliography of the writer's works, a list of additional readings, and an index of important themes and ideas.

HAROLD BLOOM

The Work in the Writer

Literary biography found its masterpiece in James Boswell's *Life of Samuel Johnson*. Boswell, when he treated Johnson's writings, implicitly commented upon Johnson as found in his work, even as in the great critic's life. Modern instances of literary biography, such as Richard Ellmann's lives of W.B. Yeats, James Joyce, and Oscar Wilde, essentially follow in Boswell's pattern.

That the writer somehow is in the work, we need not doubt, though with William Shakespeare, writer-of-writers, we almost always need to rely upon pure surmise. The exquisite rancidities of the Problem Plays or Dark Comedies seem to express an extraordinary estrangement of Shakespeare from himself. When we read or attend *Troilus and Cressida* and *Measure for Measure*, we may be startled by particular speeches of Ulysses in the first play, or of Vincentio in the second. These speeches, of Ulysses upon hierarchy or upon time, or of Duke Vincentio upon death, are too strong either for their contexts or for the characters of their speakers. The same phenomenon occurs with Parolles, the military impostor of *All's Well That Ends Well*. Utterly disgraced, he nevertheless affirms: "Simply the thing I am / Shall make me live."

In Shakespeare, more even than in his peers, Dante and Cervantes, meaning always starts itself again through excess or overflow. The strongest of Shakespeare's creatures—Falstaff, Hamlet, Iago, Lear, Cleopatra—have an exuberance that is fiercer than their plays can contain. If Ben Jonson was at all correct in his complaint that "Shakespeare wanted art," it could have been only in a sense that he may not have intended. Where do the personalities of Falstaff or Hamlet touch a limit? What was it in Shakespeare that made *Hamlet* and the two parts of *Henry IV* into "plays unlimited"? Neither Falstaff nor Hamlet will be stopped: their wit, their beautiful, laughing speech, their intensity of being—all these are virtually infinite.

In what ways do Falstaff and Hamlet manifest the writer in the work? Evidently, we can never know, or know enough to answer with any authority. But what would happen if we reversed the question, and asked: How did the work form the writer, Shakespeare?

Of Shakespeare's inwardness, his biography tells us nothing. And yet, to an astonishing extent, Shakespeare created our inwardness. At the least, we can speculate that Shakespeare so lived his life as to conceal the depths of his nature, particularly as he rather prematurely aged. We do not have Shakespeare on Shakespeare, as any good reader of the Sonnets comes to realize: they do not constitute a key that unlocks his heart. No sequence of sonnets could be less confessional or more powerfully detached from the poet's self.

The German poet and universal genius, Goethe, affords a superb contrast to Shakespeare. Of Goethe's life, we know more than everything; I wonder sometimes if we know as much about Napoleon or Freud or any other human being who ever has lived, as we know about Goethe. Everywhere, we can find Goethe in his work, so much so that Goethe seems to crowd the writing out, just as Byron and Oscar Wilde seem to usurp their own literary accomplishments. Goethe, cunning beyond measure, nevertheless invested a rival exuberance in his greatest works that could match his personal charisma. The sublime out-rageousness of the Second Part of *Faust*, or of the greater lyric and meditative poems, forms a Counter-Sublime to Goethe's own daemonic intensity.

Goethe was fascinated by the daemonic in himself; we can doubt that Shakespeare had any such interests. Evidently, Shakespeare abandoned his acting career just before he composed *Measure for Measure* and *Othello*. I surmise that the egregious interventions by Vincentio and Iago displace the actor's energies into a new kind of mischief-making, a fresh opening to a subtler playwriting-within-the-play.

But what had opened Shakespeare to this new awareness? The answer is the work in the writer, *Hamlet* in Shakespeare. One can go further: it was not so much the play, *Hamlet*, as the character Hamlet, who changed Shakespeare's art forever.

Hamlet's personality is so large and varied that it rivals Goethe's own. Ironically Goethe's Faust, his Hamlet, has no personality at all, and is as colorless as Shakespeare himself seems to have chosen to be. Yet nothing could be more colorful than the Second Part of *Faust*, which is peopled by an astonishing array of monsters, grotesque devils and classical ghosts.

A contrast between Shakespeare and Goethe demonstrates that in each—but in very different ways—we can better find the work in the person, than we can discover that banal entity, the person in the work. Goethe to many of his contemporaries seemed to be a mortal god. Shakespeare, so far as we know, seemed an affable, rather ordinary fellow, who aged early and became somewhat withdrawn. Yet Faust, though Mephistopheles battles for his soul, is hardly worth the trouble unless you take him as an idea and not as a person. Hamlet is nearly every-idea-in-one, but he is precisely a personality and a person.

Would Hamlet be so astonishingly persuasive if his father's ghost did not haunt him? Falstaff is more alive than Prince Hal, who says that the devil haunts him in the shape of an old fat man. Three years before composing the final *Hamlet*, Shakespeare invented Falstaff, who then never ceased to haunt his creator. Falstaff and Hamlet may be said to best represent the work in the writer, because their influence upon Shakespeare was prodigious. W.H. Auden accurately observed that Falstaff possesses infinite energy: never tired, never bored, and absolutely both witty and happy until Hal's rejection destroys him. Hamlet too has infinite energy, but in him it is more curse than blessing.

Falstaff and Hamlet can be said to occupy the roles in Shakespeare's invented world that Sancho Panza and Don Quixote possess in Cervantes's. Shakespeare's plays from 1610 on (starting with *Twelfth Night*) are thus analogous to the Second Part of Cervantes's epic novel. Sancho and the Don overtly jostle Cervantes for authorship in the Second Part, even as Cervantes battles against the impostor who has pirated a continuation of his work. As a dramatist, Shakespeare manifests the work in the writer more indirectly. Falstaff's prose genius is revived in the scapegoating of Malvolio by Maria and Sir Toby Belch, while Falstaff's darker insights are developed by Feste's melancholic wit. Hamlet's intellectual resourcefulness, already deadly, becomes poisonous in Iago and in Edmund. Yet we have not crossed into the deeper abysses of the work in the writer in later Shakespeare.

No fictive character, before or since, is Falstaff's equal in self-trust. Sir John, whose delight in himself is contagious, has total confidence both in his self-awareness and in the resources of his language. Hamlet, whose self is as strong, and whose language is as copious, nevertheless distrusts both the self and language. Later Shakespeare is, as it were, much under the influence both of Falstaff and of Hamlet, but they tug him in opposite directions. Shakespeare's own copiousness of language is well-nigh incredible: a vocabulary in excess of twenty-one thousand words, almost eighteen hundred of which he coined himself. And of his word-hoard, nearly half are used only once each, as though the perfect setting for each had been found, and need not be repeated. Love for language and faith in language are Falstaffian attributes. Hamlet will darken both that love and that faith in Shakespeare, and perhaps the Sonnets can best be read as Falstaff and Hamlet counterpointing against one another.

Can we surmise how aware Shakespeare was of Falstaff and Hamlet, once they had played themselves into existence? *Henry IV, Part I* appeared in six quarto editions during Shakespeare's lifetime; *Hamlet* possibly had four. Falstaff and Hamlet were played again and again at the Globe, but Shakespeare knew also that they were being read, and he must have had contact with some of those readers. What would it have been like to discuss Falstaff or Hamlet with one of their early readers (presumably also part of their audience at the Globe), if you were the creator of such demiurges? The question would seem nonsensical to most Shakespeare scholars, but then these days they tend to be either ideologues or moldy figs. How can we recover the uncanniness of Falstaff and of Hamlet, when they now have become so familiar?

A writer's influence upon himself is an unexplored problem in criticism, but such an influence is never free from anxieties. The biocritical problem (which this series attempts to explore) can be divided into two areas, difficult to disengage fully. Accomplished works affect the author's life, and also affect her subsequent writings. It is simpler for me to surmise the effect of *Mrs. Dalloway* and *To the Lighthouse* upon Woolf's late *Between the Acts*, than it is to relate Clarissa Dalloway's suicide and Lily Briscoe's capable endurance in art to the tragic death and complex life of Virginia Woolf.

There are writers whose lives were so vivid that they seem sometimes to obscure the literary achievement: Byron, Wilde, Malraux, Hemingway. But most major Western writers do not live that exuberantly, and the greatest of all, Shakespeare, sometimes appears to have adopted the personal mask of colorlessness. And yet there are heroes of literature who struggled titanically with their own eras—Tolstoy, Milton, Victor Hugo—who nevertheless matter more for their works than their lives.

There are great figures—Emily Dickinson, Wallace Stevens, Willa Cather—who seem to have had so little of the full intensity of life when compared to the vitality of their work, that we might almost speak of the work in the work, rather than even of the work in a person. Emily Brontë might well be the extreme instance of such a visionary, surpassing William Blake in that one regard.

I conclude this general introduction to a series of literary bio-critiques by stating a tentative formula or principle for gauging the many ways in which the work influences the person and her subsequent, later work. Our influence upon ourselves is always related to the Shakespearean invention of self-overhearing, which I have written about in several other contexts. Life, as well as poetry and prose, is overheard rather than simply heard. The writer listens to herself as though she were somebody else, and the will to change begins to operate. The forces that live in us include the prior work we have done, and the dreams and waking visions that evade our dismissals.

HAROLD BLOOM

Introduction

Dostoevsky's greatness is invested partly in his Nihilists—Raskolnikov, Svidrigailov, and Stavrogin—and partly in the Karamazovs, with their intense vitalism, inherited from their sublimely dreadful father. In my youth, I would have added Prince Myshkin, protagonist of *The Idiot*, but there is too much incoherence in the novel, and too much inconsistency in Myshkin, to sustain rereading in one's later years. *Crime and Punishment, The Demons* (or, *The Possessed*) and *The Brothers Karamazov* are Dostoevsky's major achievements in the novel. Dostoevsky always suffered from a sense of inferiority to Tolstoy, and envy is hardly hidden in his apparent praise of Tolstoy to the literary critic Strakhov:

> I see that you hold Leo Tolstoy in very high regard: I agree that here is much of *our own*; but not that much. And yet, *of all of us*, in my opinion, he has succeeded best in expressing more of what is us, and is thus worth talking about.

Quite aside from his substantial jealousy in regard to *War and Peace*, Dostoevsky implies that the Russian God is missing from Tolstoy, which is happily true. Presumably, *The Life of a Great Sinner*, Dostoevsky's projected novel, would have given full articulation to Dostoevsky's Great Russian messianism, so we can be grateful the book was never written. Dostoevsky was a pillar of Russian Orthodoxy: he believed that the Russian Christ would carry God to the rest of the world. Tolstoy, excommunicated by the Orthodox Church, hardly could be a larger contrast. The image of the father, for Dostoevsky, ideally was the Tsar, representative of the Russian God. Tolstoy was his own image of the father: his severely rationalized God expressed ultimately his own horror of mortality.

Ideologically and spiritually, Dostoevsky is difficult to bear: a racist Great Russian, he hated Jews, and loathed and feared the United States, which for him was only another image of the illusory freedom he called Nihilism. When Svidrigailov, in *Crime and Punishment*, is about to commit suicide, he is accosted by a little man, whose "face had the eternal expression of resentful affliction which is so sharply etched in every Jewish face, without exception." To this Jew, Svidrigailov says that he is "going to America" and then shoots himself in the forehead.

And yet the aesthetic greatness of *Crime and Punishment* and *The Brothers Karamazov* is unquestionable. Dostoevsky the novelist transcends the idolizer of the Tsar, the anti-Semite, the enemy of human freedom. The genius of Dostoevsky pragmatically was another self, distinct from the prophet of Orthodox Russian messianism. Tolstoy was essentially similar as natural man and as the seer of *War and Peace*. Dostoevsky, unlike Tolstoy, was a great parodist: it may even be said that satiric parody is the center of Dostoevsky's art. More even than powerful satire, absolute parody is a corrosive. Something in Dostoevsky is always on the verge of parodying even his own religiosity, and his worship of authority.

The best critical account of this peculiar strength in Dostoevsky is of course Mikhail Bakhtin's, whose *Problems of Dostoevsky's Poetics* demonstrates that parody is another name for Dostoevsky's dialectical polyphony, in which opposing voices are allowed full play. Still, Bakhtin's formalistic analysis applies equally well to Dickens and to Balzac, neither of whom carries parody to the border of madness, as Dostoevsky sometimes does. Something of astonishing force can break loose in Dostoevsky, as it so frequently does in Shakespeare, whose own nihilism (as I would interpret it) was a major influence upon Dostoevsky's deep, innate nihilism, as distinct from the Russian Nihilism he parodied. The daemonic, personified by Iago in Shakespeare, transcends Dostoevsky's poetics.

A.D. Nuttall, a critic who almost always persuades me, finds a borderline schizophrenia in Raskolnikov. I would prefer the older category of the daemonic, which never ceases to sustain the protagonist until the unfortunate second chapter of the "Epilogue," where love for

Sonja raises him from the dead. From start to end of the novel proper, Raskolnikov continues to believe in his Napoleonic dream of power, which reduces to the will for killing some other person, not oneself. That ought to render him dreadfully unsympathetic, but does not: the reader is seduced, despite herself, by Raskolnikov's nightmare will, by the ecstasy of trespass. Ultimately, we do not know why Raskolnikov kills, and indeed, the more he thought about it, the less Dostoevsky himself knew about it. But then, what really are Iago's motives? His direct descendant, Milton's Satan, suffers from a Sense of Injured Merit. Iago, like Satan, has been passed over for promotion. Raskolnikov has been reduced to the status of a poor student living in a cupboard, when he ought to have been Napoleon. When he murders the two old women, then he *is* Napoleon, in Dostoevsky's view.

None of us wants to be Svidrigailov, or Stavrogin, or old Karamazov, but their intensity, daemonic and unconfined, seduces us also. Dostoevsky owed immediate debts to Gogol (whom he parodied) and, to a lesser degree, to Balzac and Dickens. From Shakespeare, he learned something larger, which he successfully incarnated with savage brilliance in his grand nihilists. Bakhtin remarked that in Dostoevsky "a person's every act reveals him in his totality." That seems to me even truer of Shakespeare's persons, where outward action and psychic inwardness are uncannily fused. Whatever his ideological excesses, and despite his ignoble hatreds, the artist in Dostoevsky was Shakespeare's enlightened student.

NEIL HEIMS

Biography of Fyodor Dostoevsky

THE REFINER'S FIRE

On April 22, 1849, after reading a report by Count A.I. Orlov, the head of the Russian secret police, Tsar Nicholas I of Russia signed an order authorizing the arrest of a group of progressive writers and intellectuals. Members of the Petrashevtsy group had been gathering for several years every Friday night at the home of Mikhail Butashevitch-Petrashevsky in St. Petersburg to read aloud from their own works and from other works of current interest often forbidden by tsarist censorship. At these gatherings, too, they spoke and argued about the driving social, political, philosophical, and economic issues the censored Russian press was forbidden to mention. Their host, Petrashevsky, was author of the *Pocket Dictionary of Foreign Words*, which was not, in fact, a dictionary at all but a handbook of modern, and especially Socialist, ideas. Among those arrested was the young writer who, for a short while after the publication of his first novel, *Poor Folk*, in 1846, had been celebrated for that work and for the great literary promise it showed. In the following few years before his arrest in 1849, however, Fyodor Mikailovitch Dostoevsky, did not seem to fulfill that promise. None of his next books met with the same enthusiastic reception. Those who had praised him and supported him, notably Vissarion Belinsky, the foremost critic of his time in St. Petersburg and the foremost shaper of Russian literary taste in the 1840s, soon considered him a serious disappointment as an author. They saw him as more concerned with the psychology of aberrant individuals than with social conditions. Nor did they realize how in his novels he was showing the effects of the social on the psyche. Just as damning was the fact that Dostoevsky was awkward as a person, conceited and lacking social grace.

The orientation at Petrashevsky's Friday nights was Socialist and reformist, even revolutionary. In Russia, the absolutism of tsarist rule made even speculative discussion of socioeconomic circumstances, religious doubts and beliefs, or ameliorative philosophies dangerous. Nevertheless, the 1840s in Russia were a time of strong critical activity. The overriding issue was the liberation of the enslaved Russian peasantry, the serfs. Much of the political conversation, however, assumed a literary and cultural guise. But because of the strong climate of intellectual repression prevalent in tsarist Russia, even literary and cultural discussion was risky.

Just because a large number of educated people opposed the same things, however, did not mean they agreed about everything or even anything else. Thus inner circles formed within circles, and smaller, deeper circles were formed within those. Dostoevsky belonged to the Petrashevtsy circle and also to the Palm-Durov circle, a group which broke off from the Petrashevtsy because its members preferred to talk about literature and music rather than politics and insurgency. But within the Palm-Durov circle was an inner circle headed by Nikolay Speshnev. It used the Palm-Durov's relatively innocuous activity as a cover for its own subversive organizing of a movement whose aim was to spread insurrectionary propaganda among the serfs. At the time of the Petrashevtsy arrest, members of this inner circle, including Dostoevsky, were trying to secure a printing press and circulate clandestine propaganda.

Some time shortly after four o'clock on the morning of April 23, 1849, Dostoevsky was arrested in his bed. His door was pushed in, he was told to get dressed, his room was searched, and he was taken to the headquarters of the secret police, known as the Third Section. Joseph Frank, author of a five volume biographical study of Dostoevsky and his work, describes the scene:

> The prisoners spent all of the first day, April 23, scattered through the various rooms of the spacious headquarters of the Third Section; and they were, for some unexplained

reason, treated with a good deal of courtesy and consideration. Tea, coffee, and breakfast were served, and in the evening a carefully prepared dinner. One of the Petrashevtsy remembered even being offered cigars. (Frank, *Years of Ordeal*, 10)

From there they were removed to a comparatively comfortable section of the prison located in the Peter and Paul Fortress in St. Petersburg to await judgment.

On September 17, 1849, the Commission of Inquiry investigating the accused conspirators reported to the Tsar that they "were in general notable for a spirit of opposition to the government, and a desire to alter the existing state of things," but that they had not shown "either a unity of action or a common purpose," and that they "did not belong in the category of a secret society." It was also judged that they did not have "any sort of connection outside Russia." (*Years of Ordeal*, 49) Nevertheless, Tsar Nicholas wrote in response to Orlov's report, "I have read through it all. It's an important matter, for even if it were just a lot of idle talk, this would still be criminal and intolerable." (*Years of Ordeal*, 7) Accordingly, the investigating commission handed down decisions against 28 of the suspected conspirators. Here is the judgment brought in Dostoevsky's case:

> The Military Court finds the defendant Dostoevsky guilty of, upon receiving in March of this year from Moscow, from the nobleman Pleshcheev (a defendant), a copy of the criminal letter by Belinsky, having read this letter at meetings: first, at the home of the defendant Durov and then at the home of the defendant Petrashevsky, eventually giving it to the defendant Mombelli to be copied. Dostoevsky was at the home of the defendant Speshnev when the subversive work by the lieutenant Grigor'ev entitled "Soldiers' Conversation" was read. Hence the Military Court has sentenced him, the retired engineer-lieutenant Dostoevsky, for the failure to report the dissemination of the litterateur Belinsky's letter that constitutes criminal offense against church and government and of the pernicious work of the lieutenant Grigor'ev—to

be deprived ... of ranks, of all rights concomitant to his social
estate and to be subjected to the death penalty by shooting.
(http://www.uoregon.edu/~kimball/Petrashevtsy.htm)

This judgment was sent for review to the General-Auditoriat, the
highest military court in Russia, which added an additional charge, that
Dostoevsky had "taken part in deliberations about printing and
distributing works against the government by means of a home
lithograph." (*Years of Ordeal*, 50)

On the morning of December 22, 1849, Dostoevsky and the rest
of the Petrashevtsy were driven to Semenovsky Square in St.
Petersburg, where, in deep snow, and surrounded by a crowd of curious
onlookers, a firing squad awaited them. The first three to be shot—
Dostoevsky was among the next three—were tied to stakes on the
scaffold and blindfolded. Rifles were raised, pointed, and cocked, but
then drummers beat the signal to lower rifles and not to shoot. Several
days before, the tsar had secretly decided not to execute them but to
send them all to prison after using them in a spectacle which would
show both his might and his mercy: a last minute reprieve. It was just
the beginning of many shocks awaiting Dostoevsky in place of the firing
squad. The three who had been tied to the stake were untied. An officer
rode up to the group of the condemned and read out their punishments.
Dostoevsky's was to be four years at penal servitude (hard labor) in
Siberia followed by an indefinite period of army service. The prisoners
were then returned to the fortress. Two days later, Dostoevsky began
the arduous trip to Siberia in glacially cold weather.

During the period of his incarceration in the Peter and Paul
Fortress, before the mock execution and the years of penal servitude,
Dostoevsky was interrogated about his activities and about his
comrades. Orest Miller, Dostoevsky's first biographer, whose book
appeared in 1883, two years after Dostoevsky's death, reported that
when Dostoevsky was interrogated by one of the heads of the secret
police, General L.V. Dubelt, known always to be polite and courteous
to prisoners and even to have helped some of their families with money
of his own, and by General Y.I. Rostovtsev, General Rostovtsev said to
him, "I cannot believe that the man who wrote *Poor Folk* can be in
sympathy with these vicious people. It is impossible. You are only
slightly involved, and I am fully empowered by the Tsar to pardon you

if you agree to tell about the whole business." Dostoevsky remained uncooperative drawing forth a smile from Dubelt who said to Rostovtsev, "I told you so." But from Rostovtsev there was an explosion of rage. He screamed, "I can't bear to look at Dostoevsky," and stormed out of the room. (*Years of Ordeal*, 17) Despite this and other pressure on him, Dostoevsky revealed nothing about the work of the inner circle, which, indeed, was to determine, in the words of I.P. Liprandi, an official in the Ministry of Internal Affairs, "how to arouse indignation against the government in all classes of the population, how to arm peasants against landowners, officials against authorized superiors; how to make use of the fanaticism of the [religious] schismatics—but among other groups how to undermine and dissolve all religious feelings." (*Years of Ordeal*, 8) The truth of the charge never emerged in Dostoevsky's lifetime, but an incriminating letter, discovered in the 1920s, confirms it.

Rostovtsev's behavior, even if only an act put on to extract information, nonetheless and uncannily represented in a nutshell Dostoevsky's situation at that moment. Dostoevsky had gone from being a celebrated St. Petersburg author to a banished man whose identity was being obliterated and whose humanity would be entirely ignored. But this was only an outward change of fortune. The experience of his years of imprisonment and exile caused in him a far more profound alteration. They made him the Dostoevsky whose novels form one of the pillars of Russian literature and have defined him as one of the giants of world literature, a passionate and mystical Christian, a fervent Russian nationalist, and one of the canniest psychologists of the torments which accompany both evil and goodness.

Dostoevsky was born in Moscow on October 30, 1821, in the Mariinsky Hospital for the Poor. His father, Mikhail Andreevich Dostoevsky, was a doctor there and lived in an apartment in the hospital with his wife and their firstborn, Dostoevsky's older brother, Mikhail. Dostoevsky's father had recently been discharged from the army where he had served in the medical corps since 1812. The hospital was in the Sushchevskaya district of Moscow, an impoverished section of the city where the "cemetery for society's outcasts—tramps, suicides, criminals and their victims" was located. (Grossman, 3) Despite his position as a doctor, Dostoevsky's father was not rich. The family shared in the squalor of their surroundings, but the children also had the hospital gardens to play in, where, because of the patients also using the gardens, they had to exercise restraint.

The Dostoevskys were an old family and had belonged to the Lithuanian nobility. They had been awarded the small village of Dostoevo, from which they took their name, in the district of Pinsk, in the sixteenth century. During the course of regional conflicts between Russian (Orthodox) and Polish (Roman Catholic) religious sects over national and religious identity, the Dostoevskys fought on both sides. The Orthodox Dostoevskys lost their land and fell among the lower classes. They became, generation after generation, nonmonastic clergymen. Mikhail Andreevich, Dostoevsky's father, had also been intended by his father to be a clergyman and had been sent to a seminary. He left it, however, when he was 15, ran away to Moscow and got himself admitted to the Imperial Medical-Surgical Academy in 1809 and became a military doctor in 1812. In 1819, when he was stationed at the Moscow Hospital, Dr. Dostoevsky married Marya Feodorovna Nechaev, daughter of well-to-do merchant Fyodor Timofeevich Nechaev.

Dostoevsky's environment was full of conflict and contradiction. His mother was a gentle, obliging woman, warm and devoted to those she loved, skilled and graceful. She taught the children French and told them stories and played the guitar and sang for them. His father was a nervous, irritable, afflicted man with a passionate temper and a jealous and possessive disposition. He was guided by the desire to rise and regain his title of nobility, which he remembered his family once boasted. He was in fact restored to the nobility for his work as a medical civil servant and at once bought a small estate outside Moscow called Darvoe and soon after, the adjacent hamlet of Chermashnya. These purchases drove him heavily into debt. And they weren't very good purchases either. The estates were on poor soil, which yielded little and could not support a successful farm. His wife, however, ran the estates with an intelligent eye and a gentle hand. She made them as fruitful as she could by undertaking projects like having a series of canals dug to bring fresh water from a spring to the estate and to the peasants who lived on it. Her husband often reprimanded her for her generosity and gentleness toward the peasants. (Frank, *Seeds of Revolt*, 15) Her death in 1837, when Dostoevsky was 16, cast her husband into a mean and angry gloom, the kind to which he had always been susceptible and which only she could keep at bay. He drank heavily, was pressed for money—

partially by his son Fyodor—and acted cruelly to the peasants. In 1839, the peasants murdered him. At least that was the verdict at the time, and it was what Dostoevsky believed. Modern scholars have raised doubts about the truth of that finding. Such reservations, nevertheless, do not alter the way Dostoevsky viewed the situation or how it affected him psychologically. But he did not view his father as a villain. Even when he believed his father's plans for him were mistaken, he, nevertheless, also believed that his father had his and the family's best interest at heart. Similarly, Dostoevsky's mother kept her love for Mikhail Andreevich, even when he was abusive and accused her (without warrant) of infidelity. Writing to his brother Mikhail soon after their mother's death, Dostoevsky said:

> I feel sorry for our poor father. A strange character! Oh, how much unhappiness he has had to bear! I could weep from bitterness that there is nothing to console him. But, do you know, Papa doesn't know the world at all. He has lived in it for 50 years and retains the same ideas about people as 30 years ago. Happy ignorance! But he is very disillusioned with it. That seems our common fate. (*Seeds of Revolt*, 38)

The Dostoevsky children's first schooling was at home, provided by tutors and by their parents. Orest Miller wrote that Dostoevsky "remembered ... that they [the children] were strictly supervised and taught to study very early. At the age of four, he was already placed in front of a book and told insistently: 'Study!'" (*Seeds of Revolt*, 24) Their father taught them geometry during walks through Moscow, using the angles formed by the intersection of the streets. He also taught them Latin. He was harsh, strict, impatient, and he made them stand at attention as they recited their lessons, raged at them when they made a mistake, and often stormed out of the room in a fit of anger.

In 1833, when he was 12, Dostoevsky and his older brother, Mikhail, began attending Souchard's day school. The next year they were enrolled in Chermak's Boarding School, considered to be the best in Moscow. Dostoevsky has not left a firsthand account of what it was like in boarding school, but a description from his novel *Poor Folk*, Joseph Frank, arguably his finest biographer, believes accurately reflects his own experience:

How sad I was at first with strangers.... It was so stern, so exacting! The fixed hours for everything, the meals in common, the tedious teachers—all that at first fretted and harassed me.... I would sit over my French translation or vocabularies, not daring to move and dreaming all the while of our little home, of father, of mother, of our old nurse, of nurse's stories. (*Seeds of Revolt*, 34)

There is however an account by a younger schoolmate of Dostoevsky who had played with him in the gardens of the hospital where the Dostoevskys had an apartment. It shows the young Dostoevsky as both kindhearted and brave and also as a good storyteller:

On the first day I arrived, I gave way to a surge of childish despair on finding myself torn away from the family, surrounded by strange faces, and, as a newcomer, exposed to their taunts. During the recreation period, I heard a familiar voice among those of the children milling around me. It was that of Feodor Mikhailovitch Dostoevsky, who, on seeing me, came up at once, chased away the mocking scamps, and began to console me—which he soon succeeded in doing completely and successfully. He often visited me after that in class, guided me in my work, and lightened my sadness by his exciting stories during the recreation period. (*Seeds of Revolt*, 34–5)

Dostoevsky went home for the weekends. Initially these were pleasant times, but the sickness of his mother, which had become alarming in 1836, cast a gloom. "This was the bitterest time in the childhood period of our lives," his younger brother Andrey recalled. "We were about to lose our mother any minute. Father was totally destroyed." (*Seeds of Revolt*, 37) His father's intention to send him and Mikhail to the Academy of Military Engineers in St. Petersburg once he had decided on the career of military engineering for them was also a cause of great distress to Dostoevsky. Neither he nor his brother wished to pursue such a career—they were both devoted to literature—but their father's command had to be obeyed. In 1837, Dostoevsky's mother died in February; in May he was enrolled in Captain K.F. Kostomarov's preparatory school, and eight months later, in January 1838, Dostoevsky entered the Academy of Military Engineers. Mikhail was not accepted.

Before he left on the journey to the academy in St. Petersburg from his home in Moscow, Dostoevsky fell ill with an unidentifiable malady of the throat or chest which caused him to lose his voice. The trip was delayed until Dostoevsky's physician recommended he set out in any event and that the journey itself would prove restorative. In fact, it did. Dostoevsky regained his speech.

It was a thrilling thing to go to the great city built in the Finnish swamps by Peter the Great, a city of great bridges, monuments, and buildings, sung by the great Russian poet Pushkin, who had only four months earlier been killed in a duel. In the 1830s, St. Petersburg was the romantic center of Russia and the center of Russian literature and thought. The trip signaled a rite of passage for Dostoevsky, too, from childhood to young manhood. It also mixed longing and regret. He was beginning a career in the army, but

> [w]e dreamt only of poetry and poets. My brother [Mikhail] wrote verses, at least three poems a day even on the road, and I spent all my time composing in my head a novel of Venetian life.... My brother and I were longing for a new life, we dreamt about something enormous, about everything 'beautiful and sublime': such touching words then were still fresh, and uttered without irony. (*Seeds of Revolt*, 70)

On the trip, too, Dostoevsky saw, when they stopped at an inn, through the window in the dining room, the following scene. A government courier arrived dressed in full uniform, including a three-cornered hat decorated with white, yellow, and green plumes. The courier was powerfully built and ruddy. He stormed into the inn, downed a glass of vodka, rushed outside again and bounded into his troika. Then Dostoevsky witnessed "a sickening picture" which "remained in my memory all my life." Once in the troika, the courier stood up "and began to beat the driver, a young peasant lad, on the back of the neck with his fist. The horses lurched forward as the driver frantically whipped them." (*Seeds of Revolt*, 71) For Dostoevsky, this scene symbolized the brutal and oppressive power the Russian government exercised over the Russian people and particularly the peasantry. "This little scene," he wrote in 1876 in his *Diary of a Writer*,

> appeared to me ... as an emblem, as something very graphically demonstrating the link between cause and effect. Here every blow to the animal leaped out of each blow dealt at the man. At the end of the 1840s, in the epoch of my most unrestrained and fervent dreams, it suddenly occurred to me that, if ever I were to found a philanthropic [i.e., radical Socialist] society, I would without fail engrave this courier's troika on the seal of the society as its emblem and sign. (*Seeds of Revolt*, 72)

The conflict shaping Dostoevsky's character at this time was between an inner vision of goodness and nobility, of brotherhood and sublime awareness and an outer experience of brutality, baseness, and cynicism. His experience at the Academy of Military Engineers served to reinforce it. "I can't say anything good about my comrades," Dostoevsky wrote to his father. Twenty years later Dostoevsky remembered, "I saw children of thirteen already reckoning out their entire lives: where they could attain to what rank, what is more profitable, how to rake in cash ... and what was the fastest way to get a cushy, independent command." (*Seeds of Revolt*, 76)

In a letter to Mikhail, he described himself as "a foreign presence," and accounts of him by his schoolmates confirm that. One describes "his uniform" hanging "awkwardly, and his knapsack, shako [a high, cylindrical ornamental hat with a rising tuft of feathers], rifle—all those looked like some sort of fetters that he was obliged to wear temporarily and which weighed him down." Another, D.V. Grigorovich, who became a novelist, wrote, "already then" Dostoevsky "exhibited traits of unsociability, stayed to one side, did not participate in diversions, sat and buried himself in books, and sought places to be alone." A.I. Savelyev, who was a young officer at the academy, described Dostoevsky as "unlike the rest of his comrades.... He was very religious, and zealously performed all the obligations of the Orthodox Christian faith." His school fellows called him a monk. Savelyev further reports that Dostoevsky showed "compassion for the poor, weak and unprotected," and tried to stop the brutal hazing of incoming students by upper classmen. (*Seeds of Revolt*, 77) He displayed the same quality during his career in the army in the 1840s, when he was morally repelled at being forced to beat other soldiers as they were made to run the gauntlet. At school, he also became editor of the student newspaper and a romantic-socialist politically.

Dostoevsky did have, nevertheless, a circle of close friends, and one friend especially, with whom he shared his love for poetry and its idealism. Of Ivan Berezhetsky, a fellow student at the academy, Dostoevsky wrote to his brother in 1840, "I had a companion at my side, the one creature that I loved" with "the love of a brother." He continued in his letter to Mikhail:

> You wrote to me, brother, that I had not read [the poet and dramatist, Johann Christoph Friedrich von] Schiller. You are mistaken.... I learned Schiller by heart, talked him, dreamed him.... Reading Schiller *with him* [Berezhetsky], I verified *in him* [Berezhetsky] the noble, fiery Don Carlos and Marquis Posa and Mortimer [romantic rebels against oppressive and tyrannical rulers in two of Schiller's plays]. That friendship brought me so much sorrow and joy! ... the name of Schiller has become near and dear to me, a kind of magic sound, evoking so many memories; they are bitter, brother. (*Seeds of Revolt*, 80)

There is no further record of why memories of the friendship should be bitter for Dostoevsky. Frank speculates, using passages from Dostoevsky's *Notes from Underground*, which he argues are biographically reflective, that Dostoevsky perversely and characteristically felt disdain for his friend once Berezhetsky's devotion to him was assured.

Academically Dostoevsky did very well in school, but he was not promoted after his first year. The news was a serious blow to his father, who suffered a partial stroke upon hearing it. Dostoevsky explained the failure as an instance of ill-feelings toward him on the part of the professors at the academy. The reason, scholars now believe, for his failure to be promoted was, actually, because he got a failing grade in drill. The bad news, for Dr. Dostoevsky, was but one of the many woes he bore during the last two years of his life. After his wife died in 1837 and he had sent his sons off to be schooled in St. Petersburg, he retired from his job at the hospital, complaining of failing eyesight and rheumatism. He did not see his sons again. They did write to each other, however. He was disappointed when Mikhail did not get into the Academy of Military Engineers and that Fyodor was not awarded a scholarship and he, therefore, had to pay the tuition for him.

That was not his only expense. Dostoevsky wrote frequently asking for money. "Out in camp the most awful necessities arise," he wrote, "and without money there, you're in trouble." He spent his money on a new shako. "Absolutely all my new comrades acquired their own shakos; and my government issue might have caught the eye of the Tsar." His request seems to indicate vanity rather than necessity since he also tells his father in the letter that he was one of 140,000 men parading before the Tsar. (*Seeds of Revolt*, 84) The next spring, Dostoevsky requested funds for an additional pair of boots besides the ones issued, for buying his own tea, and for a locker for his books. "Why be an exception" [by not having these things], he wrote to his father. "Such exceptions are sometimes exposed to the most awful unpleasantness." The speciousness of his argument is exposed in the memoirs of the man who shared quarters with Dostoevsky, Count Peter Semenov, who later became a renowned explorer, geographer, and natural scientist in Russia. Semenov wrote:

> I lived in the same camp with [Dostoevsky], in the same linen tents ... and I got along without my own tea (we received some in the morning and the evening), without any more boots than I was issued, and without a trunk for my books, though I read as much as F.M. Dostoevsky. As a result, all this was not actual need but simply a desire not to be different from other comrades who had their own tea and boots and trunk. (*Seeds of Revolt*, 85)

Dostoevsky also petitioned for money to cover unexplained debts and summer expenses.

Dr. Dostoevsky always sent the money, despite how difficult it was for him because of his poor finances. But he did write telling his son of his difficulties, almost begging him to be more thrifty. The harvests had been poor, the straw roofs of the peasants' huts had to be used for fodder, and since "the beginning of spring not a drop of water, not even dew.

Heat and terrible winds have ruined everything. What threatens is not only ruin but total starvation." He concluded, imploring: "After this can you continue to grumble at your father for not sending money?" (*Seeds of Revolt*, 85) These difficulties and the absence of his wife's comforting disposition undid him. Mikhail Andreevitch was drinking heavily, he held ghostly conversations with his dead wife, was tyrannical toward his serfs, and, like Fyodor Karamazov in *The Brothers Karamazov*, took the daughter of one of the peasants as his mistress, and fathered a child with her. His death, a month after his plaintive letter, resulted, apparently, from an assault by a group of angry and rebellious serfs. The official report of the death was that Dostoevsky's father died of an apoplectic stroke.

After their father's death Dostoevsky wrote to Mikhail that he "shed many tears over the death of father," and then spoke about his own future. His father's death freed him from his father's plans for his life, and he would not stay long in the army. "My one goal is to be free. I am sacrificing everything for that. But often I think, what will freedom bring me? ... What will I be, alone in the crowd of the unkowns?" What he hoped to be was a writer and to "study 'the meaning of life and man'" because "[m]an is an enigma" which "must be solved, and if you spend all your life at it, don't say you have wasted your time; I occupy myself with this enigma because I wish to be a man." (*Seeds of Revolt*, 91)

Included in his list of "necessities" outlined in the last letter Dostoevsky wrote to his father was subscribing to a French circulating library. "How many great works of genius there are—mathematical and military genius—in the French language," he writes in defense of his request. But he was being devious, for those kinds of books were of no interest to him. It was the discourse of the day he cared about, and the prevailing literature, especially the novels of Balzac, Victor Hugo, George Sand, and Eugène Sue. Although the emphasis at the Academy of Military Engineers was on the military sciences, there were also lectures on religion, history, architecture, and French, Russian, and German language and literature. Dostoevsky attended them. He became proficient in German, studied Pushkin, Lermontov, and Russian folk poetry and was particularly attracted to French literature, the classical works of Racine, Corneille, Pascal, and Ronsard as well as the contemporary writers of French literature. In 1844, his translation of Balzac's novel *Eugènie Grandet* was published in two installments in the

Russian magazine, *Repertoire and Pantheon*. But it wasn't only school which shaped Dostoevsky's taste in literature or his sense of its importance.

When their father brought the Dostoevsky bothers to St. Petersburg in 1837 to begin their military schooling, they met Ivan Nikolaevich Shidlovsky, who was staying at the same hostel they were stopping at. Despite his being only 21, not much older than the brothers, he became a trusted friend of their father as well as of both Mikhail and Fyodor. Often Dr. Dostoevsky wrote to him about his sons and even sent money for them through him. Shidlovsky and Mikhail often enjoyed carousing together. Dostoevsky recalled him in 1873 in an interview a year after Shidlovsky's death, saying, "Mention Shidlovsky ... without fail ... he was a very important person to me then, and he deserves not to have his name sink into oblivion." (*Seeds of Revolt* 94)

Shidlovsky worked in the Ministry of Finance, but like the Dostoevsky brothers, he was devoted to literature. He wrote poetry and had an entrée into the St. Petersburg literary circles. He was an intellectual guide and mentor for Dostoevsky. Together they read the great works of literature—Homer, Shakespeare, Schiller, E.T.A. Hoffman—and discussed them. After he left St. Petersburg in 1839, Dostoevsky never saw him again, although they wrote to each other occasionally. He infused Dostoevsky with the Romantic sensibility of the time, a longing for justice in a world whose harsh realities seemed to make justice impossible, and a sense of a spiritual Ideal, of an Absolute which transcended the matter-of-factness of the daily world. At the same time he was a believer and practiced the same Russian Orthodox Christianity as Dostoevsky.

In 1801, the Emperor Paul was assassinated in a palace coup. Paul's policies had been relatively liberal. He loosened Russian control over Poland, abolished conscription and limited the power of landowners over serfs. He issued a decree on rights of succession and established procedures (ironically, considering his end) for the orderly and peaceful transfer of power from one monarch to the next. He changed Russian foreign policy from one of war with Napoleonic France to alliance with France. After his murder, his son, Alexander I, who was probably aware and even supportive of the coup, was crowned in the Kremlin on September 15. The new tsar was progressive and popular. During the first half of his reign, Alexander began formulating a plan to liberate the serfs and to allow personal civil rights to all Russians. He also broke with Napoleon and led Russia to victory in the war against Napoleon's invading Grand Army. After the Russian victory, however, Alexander did not resume his liberality, but oversaw reactionary policies of repression against liberal ideas or attempts at reform. Alexander died unexpectedly on November 19, 1825.

Despotic and brutal, Nicholas I succeeded him, continuing Alexander's harsh and repressive policies, strengthening monarchical absolutism in military and civil affairs and centralizing the Russian bureaucracy. Nicholas's first act was to punish a group of officers who attempted a rebellion—they were known as the Decembrists and the rebellion was called the Decembrist Insurrection—a month after Alexander's death, on December 14, 1825. They were aroused by the government's failure to remedy the condition of the serfs. Nicholas ordered 5 of the leaders of the mutiny shot and 31 more sent to Siberia. By this act he not only showed the power and inflexibility of the monarchy but also gave the Russian people a group of martyrs secretly to revere and, in some cases, Dostoevsky's for example, even to emulate.

The kind of romanticism Shidlovsky introduced to Dostoevsky was the dominant philosophical attitude of the 1830s in Russia. It derived from idealist German Romanticism. Its appeal in Russia was in great measure a result of the historical circumstances just outlined, which determined Russian culture and politics for most of the nineteenth century. In a repressive political climate, ideas of liberation are often metaphysical rather than social, abstract rather than practical, philosophical rather than political, romantic rather than activist. Art and philosophy rather than politics and reform were the disciplines which engaged the Russian intelligentsia when Dostoevsky became one of its members in the 1840s. Under such circumstances, thinkers can appear to be dreamers, seeking distant visions of ideal perfection. And language becomes a code for those who understand what is really being said.

There was another force, however, emerging in St. Petersburg's intellectual circles, which was both a rival and a complement to the German Idealism. It was French Social Romanticism, which did focus on the class and economic injustices, which riddled social life. This socialist vision was promulgated particularly in one of the many journals which shaped the intellectual discourse in Russia, *The Moscow Telegraph*.

It was edited by N.A. Polevoy. Polevoy also published a collection of stories in 1834 under the title *Dreams and Life*. These stories described the tension between the high ideals of his heroes, usually young artists of the lower class and the harsh actualities of real life, which sabotage their dreams and make them ridiculous. This conflict between the celestial and the terrestrial, between striving to realize transcendental ideals and coping with daily humiliations became a fundamental theme of Dostoevsky's work. In the 1840s, when he believed ardently that there were social causes for human wretchedness—emblematized by his memory of the courier beating the coachman who then furiously beat the horses—and that human improvement relied on institutional reform, Dostoevsky wove the two attitudes together. The transcendental goal was to achieve human dignity for the enslaved peasant class through recognition and reform of social evils.

Dostoevsky formed his vision of the world both from his own experience of injustice, materialism, and alienation and from literature, particularly the contemporary French authors he read and discussed with Shidlovsky. From Balzac he got the analysis of class and character as functions of each other—and, also, how in a novel to present the great tapestry of a society. From Victor Hugo he took the idea of romantic idealism in the service of social justice.

Early in his career, Dostoevsky realized that besides exploring social or metaphysical concerns, he wanted to discover and portray the Russian character. He believed in the Russian character as something apart from the essence or understanding of Europeans, and he believed that European ideas and fashions could not be imported wholesale into Russia because of the Russian people themselves. The Russian people, for Dostoevsky, were the peasants. He saw them as part of the land, and as such as having the wisdom of the soil. It had shown itself to be a Socialist wisdom in the way they organized themselves, lived, and worked communally. But the noble Russian spirit they embodied, Dostoevsky believed, was corrupt. The peasants themselves were full of vice. Their vice, however, he understood to be a result of their oppression, being bound to masters in morally dumbing slavery. Literature which dealt with the Russian character was therefore essential to him, too. Pushkin and Gogol were important for Dostoevsky because they drew the Russian character and presented its spirit. Gogol offered a realistic portrayal of pathetic character types drawn from the impoverished layer of society, but treated them with a wry distance and even ridicule. Pushkin, in Joseph Frank's characterization, dramatized

> the immense power of Petersburg to crush the lives of all those lowly and helpless folk who live in the shadow of its splendors, but ... he treats the fate of [the] poor ... with sympathy and compassion rather than with the ridicule that Gogol employs for similar types. (*Seeds of Revolt*, 136)

Dostoevsky left the army in 1844, shortly after the publication of his translation of Balzac's *Eugènie Grandet*. A year later he had written *Poor Folk* and shown it to D.V. Grigorich, a friend he had met when he was a fellow student at the academy, with whom at this time he was sharing an apartment, and who later became a novelist. Grigorich showed it to his friend Nekrasov. They were immensely excited by the book. Nekrasov was a member of a group of young literary intellectuals in St. Petersburg who formed a circle, known as the pléiade, which gathered around the influential St. Petersburg critic Vissarion Belinsky. The next day, Nekrasov showed the manuscript of *Poor Folks* to Belinsky. Belinsky, enraptured by it, through his influence elevated Dostoevsky to the empyrean of literary celebrity. But it did not last long. It was not only that those who had been moved by *Poor Folk* disliked his next pieces, but also that Dostoevsky proved clumsy in society. He could be shy and even tongue-tied. At other times, he was not restrained when he did speak, and became inflamed and argumentative. He was seen to be a mixture of self-denigration and arrogance. Dostoevsky, moreover, although he did have deep concerns about the social system and wanted to see it changed, did not cut the cloth of his novels according to the pattern of a particular fashion. Belinsky had been moved particularly by *Poor Folk* because he saw it as "the first attempt at a social novel we've [Russians] had" which "reveals such secrets of life and characters in Russia as no one before him ever dreamed of." (*Seeds of Revolt*, 138)

Dostoevsky's response to his imprisonment, from the very beginning, was heroic. He discovered his own inner depths. He was neither in despair about his lot nor merely resigned to it. He had experienced a secure Christian faith when he was about to be executed and a joy at being alive when he was reprieved. He met his punishment actively, indeed gladly, with the same sort of unflinching patience and faith which a novelist must exercise in the act of creation, which requires entering into the arduous process of discovering the depths of his characters and enduring the life-threatening, life-changing vicissitudes of fortune and the ironic designs of fate which confront them.

> ... Brother, I have not lost courage and I do not feel dispirited. Life is life everywhere, life is within ourselves and not in externals. There will be people around me, and to be a *man* among men, to remain so forever and not to lose hope and give up, however hard things may be—that is what life is, that is its purpose. I have come to realize this. This idea has now become part of my flesh and blood. Yes, this is the truth! The head that created, that lived by the superior life of art, that recognized and became used to the highest spiritual values, that head has already been lopped off my shoulders. What is left is the memories and the images that I have already created but had not yet given form to. They will lacerate and torment me now, it is true! But I have, inside me, that same heart, that same flesh and blood that can still love and suffer and pity and remember—and this, after all, is life.... good-by, brother, don't grieve for me. (Selected Letters, 51)

That's part of a letter Dostoevsky wrote to his brother after he was returned to a cell in the Peter and Paul Fortress, where he stayed another day waiting to be transported to Siberia. Like King Lear in the storm, Dostoevsky had to confront himself as "unaccommodated man," and he both accepted and transcended that condition. He found that it is enough that: "There will be people around me." He asserted that the fundamental value is "to be a man among men" no matter what the circumstances. "That," he realized is life's "purpose." Exiled though he was from society, he was not exiled from people, nor from himself, nor from life. "Life is life everywhere." A "life is within ourselves ... not in externals."

This quite astonishing strength, resolve, and sufficiency in the face of catastrophe in large part is the result of the epiphany which accompanied the mock execution: "When I turn back to look at the past," Dostoevsky wrote further on in the letter,

I think how much time has been wasted, how much of it has been lost in misdirected efforts, mistakes, and idleness, in living in the wrong way; and however I treasured life, I sinned against my heart and spirit—my heart bleeds now as I think of it. Life is a gift, life is a happiness, each minute could be an eternity of bliss.... Now at this turning point in my life, I am being reborn in another form. Brother! I swear to you that I will not lose hope and will keep my spirit and my heart pure. I shall be reborn to something better. (*Selected Letters*, 53)

What he might have taken as entombment Dostoevsky experienced as resurrection. Repeatedly he condemns the way he was, not his participation in a conspiracy against the tsar for the liberation of the serfs, but his having privileged his mind over his heart. He sees that the emotional virtues—loving, suffering, pitying, and remembering—are more fundamental than the intellectual virtues—ideas of social justice, revolutionary change, and the primacy of art—which he had served. With this new spirit guiding and protecting him, Dostoevsky began his years of penal servitude. What is, perhaps most significant is that his near-death experience brought Dostoevsky a full realization of his love of life, which he felt to be grounded in the emotions and the earth rather than in the intellect and the mind. Painful as his situation was, it made him sharply aware of that love. Although constrained, he had his life. Dostoevsky's second wife, Anna, reports that he told her years later, "That was the happiest day [when he was reprieved] of my life. I walked back and forth in my cell ... and kept singing, singing out loud—so glad I was for the gift of life." (Dostoevsky, A., 22)

In the December 22, 1849 letter, "Can it be," Dostoevsky wrote to Mikhail from his cell in the fortress,

that I shall never again take pen in hand? I hope that, in 4 years' time, it will be possible. I shall send you everything I write, if I write at all. My God! How many images to which I have given life and which are still alive will perish, will be snuffed out inside my head or will spread like poison in my blood! Yes, if I cannot write, I shall perish. Better fifteen years of confinement with a pen in my hand! (*Selected Letters*, 52)

He did not perish. He grew strong roots, invisible perhaps even to himself, but the generative source of the fruit he yet would bear. And he did manage to continue writing in prison, doing much of it in his head, but also keeping a notebook, which he could scribble in during his stays in the hospital.

His first stay in the hospital was the result of what might have been an epileptic seizure or, simply, Dostoevsky collapsed from exhaustion while shoveling snow. In the hospital Dostoevsky could sleep in a bed with a mattress—in the prison barracks the men slept on wooden planks—get nourishing food—in the barracks the men were fed a watery cabbage soup with alleged pieces of beef in it—and he was given both tea and wine. He was also away from the barracks. They were noisy, crowded, violent, filthy, freezing (although filled with the smoke from an inefficient wood stove), and stinking with the smell of men confined together and deprived of sanitary facilities. The physician in charge of the hospital, Dr. Troitsky, was a kind man who also arranged for Dostoevsky to "convalesce" in the hospital at times when an extra bed was available. It was also a medical assistant in the hospital, A.I. Ivanov, to whom Dostoevsky entrusted his forbidden notebook for safekeeping.

In *The House of the Dead*, which began to be serialized in 1860, Dostoevsky fashioned his experiences in prison into a novel. For a direct account of what he endured, we are fortunate to have the first letter he wrote after being freed from bondage. Like the last letter he wrote before being transported, it was to his brother Mikhail. It picks up where the other left off, beginning with an account of the journey to Omsk, the seat of his imprisonment. "Do you remember how we parted, my dear, my good, my beloved brother?" he writes:

> At 12 o'clock sharp ... exactly in the first minute of Christmas, I had shackles put on me the first time. They weighed 10 pounds or so and made walking extremely uncomfortable. Then they put us into open sleighs, each in a separate one with a guard.... My heart throbbed, and this made it ache and grieve dully. But the fresh air reinvigorated me ... I was in reality very calm.... [t]oward morning ... we stopped at daybreak at an inn.... We pounced on the tea as though we hadn't eaten for a whole week.... I felt very cheerful.... We were all studying ... our escort officer, and he

turned out to be a nice, kind old man, as considerate with us as is possible to imagine.... he saw to it that we were transferred to covered sleighs, which was very helpful, because at times the cold was terrible. (*Selected Letters*, 57–8)

What ought to be noticed is the sharpness and fullness of Dostoevsky's powers of observation and memory. He seems almost to be divided in two, and this division remains essential to him throughout his time incarcerated. He is the man to whom things are being done and who is being made to do things. But he is also the man, despite his suffering, who is absorbing, storing, and recounting everything, quite the way a novelist does. He describes the people he met on the way to Siberia, acts of meanness and acts of kindness, the gray coats and red sashes of the coachmen, the landscape of the villages they passed through, the character of the officers who supervised them. And his accounts are never infected with bitterness or rancor.

The commandant was a very decent man, but Drill Major Krivtsov was a scoundrel such as there are few of, a petty barbarian, a stickler for regulations, a drunk and everything repulsive one can imagine. The first thing he did was to call Durov and me idiots and promise to subject us to corporal punishment the first time we got out of line.... He always used to land on us when drunk (I never saw him sober), pick on some inmate who obviously hadn't had anything to drink, and beat him under the pretext that the man was drunk. Another time while he was making his nightly rounds, he belabored one inmate for sleeping on his right side, another for crying or talking in his sleep.... this was the man with whom I had to try to live without getting hurt. (*Selected Letters*, 59)

There were also the "hard-labor camp elements," the peasants with whom Dostoevsky was imprisoned:

They are a coarse, irritated, and embittered lot. Their hatred for the gentry passes all limits, and for this reason they displayed hostility at the sight of us, along with a malicious joy at seeing us in such sad plight. They would have devoured us if given the chance.... you can imagine for yourself how protected we were when we had to live, sleep eat, and drink side by side with these people for several years.

Dostoevsky continues depicting his community:

"You of the gentry, you've pecked at us enough with your iron beaks. You used to be a gentleman and kick people around, and now you're lower than the lowest of us"—this was the theme played to us over and over again for 4 years. 150 enemies never tired of persecuting us....the only way for us to avoid the worst of it was by meeting it with indifference, with a display of moral superiority that they couldn't fail to understand and respect in us, and by refusing to submit to their will.

This division made the inmates unable to see beyond class. Dostoevsky continued:

They had no conception of what crime we could have committed, and we ourselves kept silent about it. So they did not understand us any more than we understood them; and we had to bear the brunt of the desire to avenge, and to torment the gentry, by which these people breathe and live. (*Selected Letters*, 59)

He had seen, in his revolutionary phase, peasant failings as having social causes. Now they were actual, existential facts regardless of cause or origin. Dostoevsky's life in Siberia was one of constant threat, torment, and tension. And the ideas and ideologies, which used to explain, or seek to alter, social conditions were less than useless to him now. There was hardly a respite:

Our life was very difficult. The military forced-labor camps are tougher than the civilian. I spent the entire 4 years within the confines of the penitentiary, behind walls, except when I was sent out to work. Although the work was not always unbearably hard, there were times in rough weather, on humid days, when the mud was deep, or in winter when the cold was excruciating, when I felt at the end of my strength. Once I spent four hours doing some emergency work when the mercury froze.... My foot got frost bitten on that occasion.

If there were any kinds of relief, one was partial and infrequent—time spent in the hospital. Another was achieved through escape into a transcendental imagination, which took as its substance the events of his present fate and reformed them into art.

Dostoevsky arrived in Siberia a young Russian intellectual, well read in European literature, and a Christian Socialist dedicated to liberating the serfs. Nevertheless, his pro-European bias caused him to regard serfs as inferior in character and skill, as well as in caste, lazy and stubborn. In his heartfelt dedication to the liberation of the serfs, his intellect had guided him into an inner circle of political plotters. And he had gotten in, perhaps, deeper than he had wished to. In the months before his arrest, Dostoevsky's acquaintances perceived something gloomy and frantic. He himself referred to the man who headed his cell and had drawn him into it, Nikolay Speshnev, as a Mephistopheles. Now Dostoevsky, who had had a book put in front of him and was told to "study" when he was a boy of four, had his own fate and the penal colony he was cast into to study. He learned a great deal in Siberia because Siberia brought him to the edge of his own being and it brought him, at the same time, into contact, as an equal, with serfs, in fact, the most brutal of them. It was from his observation of the serfs that Dostoevsky came to formulate his religious and political beliefs. Dostoevsky's changed attitude toward peasants was the result of observation and of memory.

Describing the peasants at work, removing the unbroken beams of wrecked barges from the Irtish River, in *The House of the Dead*, Dostoevsky wrote,

It was totally provoking to see a sturdy crowd of stalwart men who seemed utterly at a loss on how to set to work.... as soon as they began to take out the first and smallest beam, it appeared that it was breaking, "breaking of itself," as was reported to the overseer by way of apology. (*Years of Ordeal* 129)

It bothered him to see men so inept at work. But he soon saw they were not inept at all, but that their ineptness was symptomatic. When a new overseer set an actual task (rather than a forced, incessant stream of work) for the peasants to do and told them, too, that when they finished that task, they were free to leave off work, Dostoevsky saw

> there was no trace of laziness, no trace of incompetence. The axes rang; ... to my astonishment [the beams] came up whole and uninjured. The work went like wildfire. Everyone seemed wonderfully intelligent all of a sudden.... the convicts went home tired but quite content. (*Years of Ordeal*, 129)

He realized that the peasants were *made* lazy and inept by the oppression of never-ending and meaningless toil, but that when the task was defined and left up to them to do and they could see an end to their labor, they worked well. He also learned to appreciate the Russian culture which the peasants embodied. By the intellectuals of the day, Russian culture was held as less worthy than Western European culture. In Siberia, Dostoevsky heard the peasants perform on their own instruments and act in plays they produced. In this way he saw the depth, meaning, and authenticity of the Russian spirit. It caused him to cast off the contempt for Russian culture shared by the pro-Western St. Petersburg intelligentsia. Joseph Frank reports, for example, that the critic Belinsky

> consistently denigrated all attempts to assign any value to [Russian] folk poetry, and declared of Pushkin's "The Bridegroom" that "in all Russian folk songs taken together there is not more of the folk essence than in this one ballad." ... folk material had to be filtered through a sophisticated Russian European sensibility in order to take on any true literary quality. (*Years of Ordeal*, 130)

But after hearing the peasant band composed of violins, balalaikas, guitars, accordions, and a tambourine play, Dostoevsky, who had attended concerts regularly, wrote:

I had no idea till then what could be done with the simple peasant instruments. The blending of harmony and sounds, above all, the spirit, the character of the conception and rendering of the tune in its very essence were simply amazing. For the first time I realized all the reckless dash and gaiety of the gay dashing Russian dance songs. (*Years of Ordeal*, 130)

Seeing the peasant theatricals performed in prison gave him a similar impression. He was moved by the authenticity of their characterization, free of the insincerity of Western stylization.

Perhaps more than any other experience of the peasants in Siberia, one, which occurred on an Easter Monday, is pivotal in the evolution of Dostoevsky's regard for and connection to the Russian peasantry. Because it was Easter, the convicts were given a two-day holiday from their work, and they spent their leisure in drunkenness and brutality. Unable to tolerate the horrors of the fighting and the beatings, Dostoevsky left the barracks. One of the Polish political prisoners passing Dostoevsky muttered, "I hate these bandits," in French. Although these words gave utterance to what were Dostoevsky's feelings at that moment, too, their effect on Dostoevsky was quite the opposite. He immediately returned to the barracks, lay down on his plank bed with his hands under his head and spontaneously remembered an episode from his boyhood. He had been playing joyfully in the woods on his father's estate when startlingly he experienced an auditory hallucination, hearing the warning cry of "wolf" being shouted. He fled from the woods in panic and was stopped by one of his father's peasants, a coarse man named Marey, who treated Dostoevsky with a great gentleness and calmed his hysteria. The effect of this recalled act of loving kindness was that Doestoevsky

got off the plank bed and gazed around.... I suddenly felt I could look on these unfortunates with quite different eyes, and suddenly, as if by a miracle, all hatred and rancor had vanished from my heart. I walked around, looking attentively at the faces that I met. That despised peasant with the shaven head and brand marks on his face, reeling with drink, bawling out his hoarse, drunken song—why, he may be that

very Marey, after all, I am not able to look into his heart.
(*Years of Ordeal*, 123)

Although Dostoevsky's understanding of Russian peasants was
changing, the peasants' attitudes toward him remained for a long time
defined by class hostility. It was only by their slow apprehension of his
character as an individual did their prejudice against him abate and did
he gain their good will as they perceived him to be a "good man." (*Years
of Ordeal*, 133) His prison experience with the peasants changed his
political thinking. Beneficent social change, Dostoevsky came to believe,
was the result of a revolution in the human disposition, not in the
political structure. That did not mean that Dostoevsky no longer desired
freeing the serfs. He still did. Nor that he did not support social and
economic improvements and freedom of expression. He did. He had
seen for himself how the peasants worked well when they could
command themselves and had good hope of respite when their task was
accomplished. But underlying everything for him in importance was the
quality of the human being, which he believed, although shaped by social
circumstances, was still not bound by them. And this human quality, too,
he learned to define by what he saw in the treatment of the prisoners by
their jailers and by the response of the peasants to their ill-treatment.
Seeing discipline maintained by flogging and other such brutality led
Dostoevsky to conclude in *The House of the Dead* first that

> [a]nyone who has once experienced this power, this
> unlimited mastery of the body, blood and soul of a fellow
> man made of the same clay as oneself, a brother in the law of
> Christ—anyone who has experienced this power and full
> license to inflict the greatest humiliation upon another
> creature made in the image of God will unconsciously lose
> the mastery of his own sensations.... [T]he very best men may
> be coarsened and hardened into a brute by habit. [4:15] (*Years
> of Ordeal*, 150)

What became especially important for Dostoevsky, however, was
the response he saw in several peasants to the never-ending brutality and
oppression. Their religious absorption was strong and gave them
transcendent strength, a kind of mystical power of the will. Dostoevsky

himself had never abandoned his own Russian Orthodox Christian faith even as a revolutionary. He saw Christ as an idea and an ideal. In prison he came to see Christ as a force within each person. The Russian people, it seemed to Dostoevsky, Joseph Frank argues

> had absorbed the ideal of the crucified and humiliated Christ—the kenotic ideal so typical of Russian Christianity, which (according to G.P. Fedotov in *The Russian Religious Mind*) is founded on "the evaluation of suffering as a superior moral good, as almost an end in itself." (*Years of Ordeal*, 158)

The ideal the Russian peasant came to embody for Dostoevsky was a suffering as steadfast as the Russian land itself. The land was the source of the Russian spirit if the Russian people stayed close to it, as the serfs did. If they did not stay close to it, they lost their spirit and became materialists and risked denying the existence of God and leaving man to imagine himself as God. The consequence of leaving the authentic lowness of the land was that men chose power over suffering. But it was the exercise of power and the rejection of suffering—in effect a rejection of Christ—which Dostoevsky saw as the cause of mankind's grief. The political arguments in which Dostoevsky would participate in the 1860s and the themes which occupied his great novels were born during his prison years.

The Survivor's Response

Released from imprisonment, and the shackles removed from his limbs, Dostoevsky moved one step closer to freedom but nevertheless did not become a free man. According to his sentence, he had to serve an indefinite period as a common soldier. "[I]n the overcoat of a soldier, I am just as much of a prisoner as before," he wrote to Natalya Fonvizina, the wife of a Decembrist. She was one of the women who followed their husbands into exile and sought also to bring comfort to newly convicted political prisoners. Dostoevsky had met her on his journey to Siberia. She had given him 10 rubles and a New Testament, which he kept with him during his four years in prison. He often read from it, and from it he taught a fellow convict to read.

As a soldier, Dostoevsky was assigned to the 7th Line Battalion of the Siberian Army Corps, stationed in Semipalatinsk, a city in the Asian sector of the Russian Empire, far from St. Petersburg. As an ex-convict, he was permitted to take up his writing again, but not permitted to publish it. The years between his release from his chains in 1854 and his return to St. Petersburg in 1860 were, for him, a period of campaigning to regain the right to live in St. Petersburg and the right to publish.

In 1855 Tsar Nicholas I died and Alexander II came to the throne. Russia was engaged in the Crimean War, fighting against England, France, and Turkey. Dostoevsky wrote to his brother Mikhail imploring him to petition the tsar to transfer him from his regiment in Siberia to active duty in the Russian army in the Caucasus. By serving in combat Dostoevsky hoped he might show his loyalty to the tsar and increase his chances of being pardoned and having his right restored to live in St. Petersburg and to have his work published. He even put his pen in the service of his restoration. In May 1854, he submitted a patriotic war poem, "On European Events in 1854," through the commander of his battalion, Lieutenant-Colonel Belikhov, to the chief of staff, Lieutenant-General Yakovlev for publication in the *St. Petersburg Gazette*. It wasn't printed. Lost in the archives of the secret police, it was discovered there in 1883, two years after Dostoevsky's death. A year later, in 1855, after the death of Nicholas I, Dostoevsky wrote another ingratiating, patriotic poem, "On the First of July, 1855," addressed to the deceased tsar's widow celebrating her birthday. This time, Dostoevsky's poem did succeed in accomplishing what it was intended for. His friend and confidant, Baron Wrangel, asked the Governor-General of Semipalatinsk, a man named Gasfort, to forward the poem to the empress, which he did. Wrangel, in his memoirs tells a more colorful version of the event. He says he showed the poem to his children's music teacher, the piano virtuoso, Adolphe Henselt, who had friends among the music lovers in the widowed empress's entourage. In any case, the poem actually did reach the empress. Dostoevsky was rewarded by a promotion to the rank of *unter-ofitser* in November 1855. (*Years of Ordeal*, 203)

Dostoevsky also asked his brother to send him books. They had been forbidden in prison under the harsh rule of the brutal Major Krivtsov, but even after Krivtsov had been replaced, the bitterness of his estrangement from his literary career made reading difficult for Dostoevsky. Now in Semipalatinsk, Dostoevsky requested books on history, economics, politics, and philosophy. He especially wanted a

German dictionary, thinking that the way to reenter the profession of writing was through translating other writers' works. But Dostoevsky was at work on several things of his own, too. The most important of them was his novelistic account of life in prison, *The House of the Dead.*

Dostoevsky most needed time by himself so that he could write. Barracks life, however, was made particularly trying by his company sergeant, who enjoyed harassing him. Nevertheless, Dostoevsky had influential friends, especially Konstantin Ivanov and his wife. Ivanov was the son-in-law of another of the self-exiled wives of the transported Decembrists. Through the intercession of the Ivanovs and several of their friends in the higher levels of the army in Semipalatinsk, Dostoevsky did obtain permission to live by himself in town. (*Years of Ordeal*, 178) Dostoevsky also became acquainted with the more intellectual members of the Russian community in Semipalatinsk who found it interesting to have an ex-convict and a once well-known novelist in their midst. He became tutor to many of their children and in that way became a familiar figure in their homes. Mme. Stepanova befriended him, and so, consequently, did her husband, the company commander, who had been posted in Siberia because of his habitual drunkenness. He showed Dostoevsky the verses he wrote and asked him to correct them. Dostoevsky also became friendly with his battalion commander, Lieutenant-Colonel Belikhov, who employed Dostoevsky to read out loud to him from newspapers and journals. Often after Dostoevsky's reading, Belikhov invited him to stay to dinner. It was at Belikhov's that Dostoevsky met Alexander Ivanovich Isaev and his wife, Marya Dmitrievna, who was to become Dostoevsky's wife several years later in February 1857.

Alexander Ivanovich had lost his position as a schoolmaster because he was a drunkard. He found a position as a customs official in Siberia, but he was not able to keep that either. What little money he did earn was lost in drinking with unsavory companions, and the Isaevs led an impoverished life in Semipalatinsk, cut off from their respectable neighbors by his debauchery. Dostoevsky, after Isaev's death, however, writing to Mikhail, spoke kindly of him, saying Isaev "suffered from much undeserved persecution at the hands of local society," and "was as careless as a gypsy, self-centered, proud, but ... could not discipline himself.... And yet," Dostoevsky concludes, "he was highly cultivated and the kindliest of persons." (*Years of Ordeal* 180)

Soon, Dostoevsky and Isaev's wife were lovers. Much of the knowledge we have of their affair comes from the letters Dostoevsky wrote to Baron Wrangel. And much comes from the letters Dostoevsky and Marya exchanged, especially after her husband managed to secure a post in Kuznetsk, which Frank describes as "a miserable backwater lost in the depths of the Siberian wilderness." The Isaev's were so destitute that Dostoevsky had to give them the money for the journey despite his own poverty and despite his resentment that Marya had not chosen to stay with him. Wrangel reports that Dostoevsky told him, "she doesn't object [to leaving], that's what's so shocking." Dostoevsky and Wrangel accompanied the Isaevs on the first leg of their journey, and Dostoevsky and Marya took a lovers' farewell while Wrangel distracted her husband with champagne. (*Years of Ordeal*, 200)

When Dostoevsky met her in 1854, according to Wrangel,

> Marya Dmitrievna was about thirty years old, a quite pretty blonde of medium height, very slim, with a passionate nature given to exalted feeling. Even then an ill-omened flush played on her pale face, and several years later tuberculosis took her to the grave. She was well-read, quite cultivated, eager for knowledge, kind, and unusually vivacious and impressionable. She took a great interest in Dostoevsky and treated him kindly, not, I think, because she valued him deeply, but rather felt sorry for an unhappy human being beaten down by fate. It is possible that she was even attached to him, but there was no question of being in love. (*Years of Ordeal* 180–1.)

Wrangel's assessment seems to have been accurate. After Marya left Semipalatinsk, she and Dostoevsky continued their stormy liaison by correspondence:

> I have never considered our meeting an ordinary one [he wrote], and now, deprived of you, I have understood many things. I lived for five years deprived of human beings, alone, having nobody, in the full sense of the word, to whom I could pour out my heart.... The simple fact that a woman held out her hand to me has constituted a new epoch in my life.... The

heart of a woman, her compassion, her interest, the infinite
goodness of which we do not have an idea, and which often
... we do not even notice, is irreplaceable. I found all that in
you. (*Years of Ordeal*, 201)

Or perhaps, rather, he placed them in her and his love was a desire
desperate for an object. Five years in the house of the dead caused great
need and desperation, too. Marya, for example, was a person with an
explosive temper. Dostoevsky turned a disturbance into a virtue. He saw
her as ennobled by being "offended by the fact that a filthy society did
not value or understand you." And he adds, idealizing her, that "for a
person with your force of character it is impossible not to rebel against
injustice." (*Years of Ordeal*, 201)

But her behavior and her letters show her as capricious,
manipulative, and perhaps even sadistic, rather than straightforward and
forceful. After her departure, her letters were more frequently a source
of torment than of joy, especially when she wrote extensively extolling
the virtues of a young schoolteacher, a friend of her husband, whom she
had met. (*Years of Ordeal*, 202) When Baron Wrangel arranged a meeting
between her and Dostoevsky at a point between Semipalatinsk and
Kuznetsk, she failed to show up, sending a letter of excuse in her place.
After her husband's death in 1855, Dostoevsky had even more reasons
for his overwhelming desire to be allowed to publish. It would put him
in a position to be able to propose marriage to her. But she wrote to him
of other offers of marriage, which cast gloom upon him, especially when
she wrote, he told Baron Wrangel, without reference to "our future
hopes, as if that thought had been completely put aside," and asking him,
instead, how he would feel if she were to get an offer of marriage from a
man "of a certain age with good qualities, in the service, and with an
assured future[.]" (*Years of Ordeal*, 205) But this was a ruse, Dostoevsky
learned later, which he excused in a subsequent letter to Wrangel:

Basing herself on something that had really happened, she
wrote to me: "How should she reply if someone asked her
for her hand?" If I had answered with indifference, she
would have had proof that I had really forgotten her. When
I received that letter I wrote a desperate one, terrible, which
tore her apart, and then another. She had been ill these last

days; my letter really finished her off. But it seems that my despair was sweet to her, although she suffered for me.... I understand her: her heart is noble and proud. (*Years of Ordeal*, 207)

Dostoevsky was convinced that she did love him and he asked her not to make any decisions regarding remarriage until her year of mourning was completed. In the meantime, he redoubled his efforts to liberate himself from army service. Taking the risk of violating army regulations, Dostoevsky sent a letter through Baron Wrangel to General E. I. Totleben (how uncanny that the first syllable of the name suggests the German word for "death" and the second, the word in that language for "life"). Totleben was at that moment a national hero in Russia because of his military service in the defense of Sevastopol in the ongoing Crimean War. Dostoevsky wrote:

I was guilty. I recognize it fully. I was convicted of having the intention (but only that) of acting against the government; I was condemned legally and justly; a long tribulation, torturing and cruel, sobered me up and changed my ideas in many ways. But then—then I was blind, believed in theories and utopias.... Previously I had been ill for two years running, with a strange moral sickness.... There were even times when I lost my reason. I was excessively irritable, impressionable to the point of sickness, and with the ability to deform the most ordinary facts and give them another aspect and dimension. (*Years of Ordeal*, 206)

Dostoevsky condemns himself as having been like a drunkard, corrupted by an ill-functioning intellect and deranged by a moral sickness. His argument for social resuscitation is that he has been "sobered up" by his punishment. The letter accomplished its purpose. Totleben agreed to intercede for Dostoevsky with the Ministry of War and requested that Dostoevsky either be promoted to ensign or released from the army and transferred to the lowest rank of the civil service. In either case, according to the law, Dostoevsky would regain the right to publish. In the fall of 1856, Dostoevsky was promoted and became a commissioned officer.

Besides having the right to publish, Dostoevsky now also had the means to marry. But there were still obstacles to marrying, not, to be sure, erected by the tsar's government, but by Dostoevsky's beloved. Dostoevsky and Marya had agreed she would join him in Barnul, a town located in the mining district of the Altai region. But she changed her mind, writing him a letter with "flashes of tenderness," interlaced with protestations "that she could not make me happy, that we are both too unhappy, that it would be better for us ..." The rest of the letter does not survive because Dostoevsky's second wife, Anna, ripped up its remaining pages when she organized his papers after his death. (*Years of Ordeal*, 209) Dostoevsky's response to Marya's break with him was to rush to Kuznetsk to see her. There he discovered that she had another lover, a 24-year-old schoolmaster. Dostoevsky used all his power with words to convince her that a marriage with a man much younger than herself would be a disaster. She wept at his words and told him nothing was decided. Dostoevsky met Nikolay Vergunov, her young lover. He cried too, increasing the welter of emotion. Dostoevsky wrote to Wrangel to see if he could secure a better post for Vergunov. If Marya must marry him, he wrote to Wrangel, she ought not to suffer poverty.

After considerably more of this melodrama, Marya finally married Dostoevsky on February 7, 1857. It was not a happy union, and it began badly. On the way back to Semipalatinsk from Kuznetsk where the marriage was celebrated, Dostoevsky wrote to his brother Mikhail, the newlyweds "stopped in Barnul, at the home of one of my good friends. And then misfortune came my way; totally unexpectedly, I had an attack of epilepsy, which frightened my wife to death, and filled me with sadness and dejection." (*Years of Ordeal*, 214) He also learned there that the fitful disturbances he had endured since his days in Siberia, "contrary to everything said previously by doctors," were attacks of "*genuine epilepsy*, and that I could expect, in one of these seizures, to suffocate because of throat spasms and would die from this cause." The doctor could only advise that Dostoevsky "be careful at the time of the new moon." (*Years of Ordeal*, 216) Dostoevsky's daughter by his second marriage, Lyubov, reports in her memoirs that Marya continued to see Vergunov, as a lover, after her marriage, and that she not only told Dostoevsky so, but further taunted him with descriptions of how they laughed at his cuckolding. Joseph Frank, a thoroughly scholarly and reliable biographer of Dostoevsky, argues, however, that Lyubov's accounts of her father's life are highly unreliable and cannot corroborate her. Whether or not Marya was unfaithful to him, Dostoevsky was unfaithful to her, and the marriage was full of discord, rancor, and scolding. In a letter to his brother Mikhail, Dostoevsky writes,

> My wife greets you. She wrote to Varinka and Verochka [Dostoevsky's sisters], but neither replied. This is very bitter for her. She says that this means you are angry with her, and do not desire her in the family. I affirm the opposite, but in vain.... She is very unhappy. (*Years of Ordeal*, 218)

A year later, he wrote Mikhail, "My life is hard and bitter." To Baron Wrangel he wrote, "I have burdened myself with the cares of a family and I pull them along." (*Years of Ordeal*, 219) Marya died of tuberculosis on April 15, 1864. Much of their time together was spent apart.

Dostoevsky applied for permission to resign from the army at the beginning of 1858. He had already begun writing again but was uneasy about whether he would be allowed to publish and earn his living by writing. He was also concerned about his epilepsy, and he listed as the reason for his request his desire to go to St. Petersburg to consult specialists. The resignation took effect in May 1859. In July, Dostoevsky began the return journey to St. Petersburg. He crossed through the Ural Mountains on the way out of Asia and back to Europe. At the border Dostoevsky alighted from his carriage, "and I crossed myself; God, at last, had led me to the promised land.... Then we took out our plaited flask full of tangy wild-orange brandy ... and we drank our goodbye to Asia." (*Years of Ordeal*, 290–1) Once he was in European Russia, the way to St. Petersburg was neither straight nor swift. Dostoevsky had to wait in Tver during negotiations by his high-ranking friends for permission to live in St. Petersburg. Dostoevsky finally arrived in St. Petersburg at the end of December in 1859 to begin his life as a public man again.

To be a public man for Dostoevsky meant placing himself inside the social, political, and religious arguments, which made up the political and intellectual life, and affected the historical course, of Russia. Those arguments were presented and developed in a number of journals published in St. Petersburg and Moscow. The issues and ideas debated grew out of the social conditions of the Russian people. The journals they were debated in existed because the first years of Alexander's reign saw a relaxation of the restrictions on the open exchange of ideas, which had been enforced under Nicholas. Alexander abolished serfdom. And he presided over Russia's defeat in the Crimean War. These events created a social ferment, which Alexander permitted while, nevertheless, keeping a sharp eye on it through the secret police. By a letter from the military governor-general of St. Petersburg to the St. Petersburg chief of police, for example, we learn that the tsar ordered Dostoevsky to be kept under surveillance.

In prison Dostoevsky learned to surrender to the world as it was and then to transcend it through a strong, mystic, Christian faith in God and eternity. His intellectual and spiritual transformation did not remove his concern about the social issues that had absorbed him before his imprisonment. He still wanted to explain the causes of the ills people endured or inflicted and he still was devoted to find the way of eradicating those ills and eliminating their causes. The arguments Dostoevsky engaged in with himself and with others, although they were political, gave rise to cogitations which were often psychological and spiritual. Dostoevsky developed in prison, as we have seen, a sense that the Russian peasantry had an organic connection to the Russian land and a Christian faith which was not a mere intellectual construct, but which was rooted in that land. Similarly, the Russian peasantry had a stubborn power of endurance and suffering. This characteristic, more than being a virtue, was a spiritual model; weakness, Dostoevsky believed, is greater than strength. Being weak is the perfect imitation of the crucified Christ, the suffering God, who by suffering, transcended the causes and conditions of suffering. By not opposing the causes or agents of suffering, one avoids inflicting harm on others and avoids ideas and feelings of enmity, violence, or vengeance. In order to transcend the oppression of the world, in Dostoevsky's experience, one must transcend oneself.

This line of thought was particularly important to Dostoevsky during the years of the 1860s. Revolutionary Nihilism had captured the spirit of the young, and a materialist Socialism—different from the Socialism founded on Christian attitudes to which Dostoevsky and many of the young intellectuals had been devoted in the 1840s—was the prevailing doctrine among a good many of the intellectuals. The conversion Dostoevsky experienced in Siberia was not with regard to religious belief. He was always a believer. It was about Man's responsibility for the way things are. Before imprisonment, Dostoevsky wanted to see a revolution in the way society was structured. During imprisonment he began to believe that there had to be a revolution in the human disposition before there could be any significant and worthwhile change in social structures. He no longer saw social institutions as the fundamental cause of evil. He accepted the Christian view of mankind as having an original, inherent, and defining culpability. The role of Christ, then, is not to serve as a model for noble behavior but as a Savior. (*Years of Ordeal*, 289)

In 1861 Alexander II liberated the serfs. His intention to do so had been known since the middle 1850s. When Dostoevsky returned to St. Petersburg mid-December 1859, he returned to a place quite different from the one in which he had been arrested. Many exiles were returning because of the liberal climate, which would not last beyond a few more years. There was little of the tension of rebellion Dostoevsky had known before his arrest in 1849. The new tsar had gained the love of the people by his enlightened policies, particularly by the liberation of the serfs. Dostoevsky remained devoted to Tsar Alexander II throughout his life.

Dostoevsky was met at the station by his brother Mikhail, who had rented an apartment for him, his new wife, and her son, now Dostoevsky's ward, Pasha. The night of their arrival, the apartment was the scene of a gathering celebrating his return. Many old friends from the Petrashevtsy circle, and a few from more inner and secret circles, were present, including Nikolay Speshnev, just back from Siberia himself, whom Dostoevsky had called his Mephistopheles, the devil who tempted him to illegal political action. Alexander Milyukov was also present. He had been a member of the Palm-Durov circle with Dostoevsky, but not of the inner group, the Speshnev conspiracy, for which it had served as a front without its members knowing it. Milyukov had not been arrested, and now was the editor of a literary magazine called *The Torch* and was the center of a circle himself. He invited Dostoevsky to attend his Tuesday nights. Dostoevsky did and found himself quickly reintegrated into the literary-intellectual life of St. Petersburg, not least because he had endured a ten-year exile. Seeing him read publicly from *Netochka Nezvanova*, the novel Doestoevsky had been writing at the time of arrest, the diarist Elena Shtakenschneider wrote: "Certainly we will consider everything for which he suffered to be truth, though I do not really know very well what he suffered for; enough that he suffered." (Frank, *Stir of Liberation*, 14)

Dostoevsky had begun to write again soon after release from prison in 1854. In 1857, "A Little Hero," unsigned, appeared in a Russian periodical. "Uncle's Dream" and "The Village of Stepanchikovo" were rejected by several publications, but finally appeared in 1860. These works were accounted failures when they first appeared, nor have they achieved a reputation over time as, for example, *The Double* has, although when it appeared after *Poor Folk* it was greeted with scorn. In 1860, a two-volume edition of Dostoevsky's work was published. But Dostoevsky, upon his return from exile was not celebrated simply because of what he had undergone. In 1860, he began working on two new projects. With the serialization of *Notes from the House of the Dead* beginning in the September 1860 edition of *Russky Mir (Russian World)* and *The Insulted and the Injured*, beginning in *Vremya (Time)* in January 1861, Dostoevsky reestablished himself as a writer of real importance. Publishing in *Time* had added significance. Dostoevsky not only reemerged as a formidable novelist, but also as one of the editors of what would be for two years an important monthly journal, until it was shut down by imperial censorship in May 1863.

During the 1850s Mikhail Dostoevsky, who maintained a minor literary career publishing essays and translations in the journals, wrote to his brother in exile that they ought to edit their own magazine. During his brother's imprisonment he had also bought and run a small cigarette factory. When Dostoevsky returned to St. Petersburg, therefore, because of the cigarette factory, Mikhail could finance a magazine, and the brothers started *Time*.

Several days after his return to St. Petersburg, Dostoevsky was elected to the board of the Society for the Aid of Needy Writers and Scholars, generally known as the Literary Fund. As its name suggests, the task of the society was to raise money and give grants to indigent writers, and scholars. It also provided aid to scholars, writers, and students who were arrested on political grounds and who were, therefore, unable to support themselves and their families. Thus Dostoevsky saw to it that the fund helped a number of people whose political views he himself no longer supported. As a member of the Literary Fund, Dostoevsky participated in public readings to raise money and, between 1863 and 1865, Dostoevsky held the office of

Secretary of the Administrative Committee. In this capacity he kept records of the meetings of the Literary Fund and took care of all correspondence. These were activities Dostoevsky pursued in addition to his writing, of course, and set against the background of his tempestuous personality, his melodramatic and far from happy family life, and his several and often painful extra-marital love affairs. There was also his epilepsy, a violent, unpredictable disease erupting whenever it would and leaving its traces after the attack in lingering pain and disorientation, but whose onset produced feelings of great bliss.

Dostoevsky did not lose his fierce attachment to social issues or to a vision of The Good during his imprisonment. He reoriented himself, but he never altered his fundamental beliefs in human brotherhood and cooperation. Only his understanding of what form these ideals could take and how they might be achieved changed. With the publication of *Time*, he introduced his revised *Weltanschauung* into the arena of public thought and debate. The underlying philosophy of *Time* and of *Epokha (Epoch)*, its successor in 1864, was *pochvennichestvo*, a doctrine emphasizing the importance of the Russian soil as the foundation of Russian life. It emphasized the difference between Slavic and European ways of thinking and living, arguing for the Slavic, calling for Russians to return to their native soil and to value their culture rather than try to imitate Europe. The basics of Russian culture, as Dostoevsky had understood them in prison, and whose dissemination became a widespread social goal by the early 1860s, could be found in the attitudes and customs of the Russian peasants. Foremost was a religious piety derived from a mystical and spiritual way of understanding rather than a rational and materialist way. Indicting himself and the activists of the 1840s, Dostoevsky wrote, "Everything ... was done according to principle, we lived according to principle, and were terribly afraid to do anything not in conformity with the new ideas." (*Stir of Liberation*, 58)

Dostoevsky did not, however, blindly idealize the peasantry. He campaigned in *Time* for the education of the serfs and for universal literacy among them. He argued that without universal literacy, those peasants who can read become disdainful of the others who cannot. Consequently, they become alienated from the essential common humanity found in being able to identify with, rather than scorn, the peasantry.

The climate of debate, which Dostoevsky entered in 1860, by the middle of the decade had become a climate of violence. Dostoevsky had maintained sympathy for the philanthropic socialist materialists even while he thoroughly disparaged their beliefs because he believed in the goodness of their motives despite their misguided or even ill-guided methods. Rather than condemn them, in his writing in *Time* he tried to warn them that their actions were ill-advised and could not have a beneficial outcome. Dostoevsky kept that attitude with the advent of the Nihilists, but he was much more troubled with them because of their open adherence to violence. Dostoevsky proclaimed a philosophy of loving transcendence of the social evil. The way, he believed, we transcend the current evil is by accepting suffering. Such acceptance is a spiritual act that joins mankind together. Accepting suffering, Dostoevsky believed, robs those who inflict it of their power. And it helps, he believed, those who undergo suffering to overcome by chastisement, the sinfulness which is, he believed, inherent to human nature. The Nihilists rejected suffering. They wanted to gain and use power to overthrow power.

On June 7, 1862, Dostoevsky set out on his first trip to Europe. A year earlier, he had written to the Russian poet Y. P. Polonsky who was traveling in Europe:

> How many times, starting with the days of my childhood, have I dreamed of being in Italy. Ever since the novels of Ann Radcliff, which I read when I was eight years old, all sorts of Catarinas, Alfonos, and Lucias have been running around in my head.... Then it was the turn of Shakespeare—Verona, Romeo and Juliet—the devil only knows what magic was there. Italy! Italy! but instead of Italy I landed in Semipalatinsk, and before that in the Dead House. Will I ever succeed in getting to Europe while I still have the strength, the passion and the poetry? (*Stir of Liberation*, 180)

A year later, he wrote his brother Andrey to tell him that he was going to Europe without Marya, his wife, who was staying in Russia to help guide her son through his entrance examination to the *gymnasium*. He said he was going principally for medical treatment. (*Stir of Liberation*,

180) At the Russian-German border, he later wrote in his account of the journey, *Winter Notes on Summer Impressions*, he thought,

> And so I am at last going to see Europe, I, who have so vainly dreamt about it for almost forty years, I, who when I was sixteen, very seriously, "wished to Switzerland to flee," ... but did not flee; and now at last I am about to enter "the land of holy wonders," the land I had so often longed for and languished after, in which I had placed so stubborn a faith! [5:51] (*Stir of Liberation*, 181)

He was going in order to test that faith. It had been from Europe that he had gotten his early Socialist ideal and an ideal of culture, but his years in prison had relocated him in Russia and given him a new regard for Russian values. Dostoevsky developed a philosophy deeply grounded in transcendence through renunciation—essential in prison. Rationalist Europe, on the other hand, offered him a place for license. It was in Europe that he allowed himself compulsive gambling. He did not gamble in Russia. Rather than being a disease, gambling was a behavior associated with a particular location. Europe offered him a destructive freedom; Russia, a liberating bondage. It was bred into his bone in Russia that if he wanted to live and be himself, he would have to learn the severity of strong discipline and agree to a constraint that he was not free to oppose. He had worn iron for four years: movement wasn't free; being fettered had become a corporeal memory. Europe was where the constraints did not apply.

Europe represented one of the terms in a conflict which occupied Dostoevsky, in various forms, throughout his life. It was a conflict of loyalties between Europe and Russia, between freedom and obedience, between intellect and emotion, between rationality and passion, between materialism and spirit, ultimately, between parts of himself. Varvara Timofeyeva, who worked with Dostoevsky when he was editing *The Citizen*, describes Dostoevsky's struggle as it expressed itself in his physiognomy. He had, she writes,

> a gloomy, exhausted face, covered like a net with some sort of unusually expressive shadings caused by a tightly restrained movement of the muscles. As if every muscle on this face

with sunken cheeks and a broad high forehead was alive with feeling and thought. And *these feelings and thoughts were irresistibly pushing to come to the surface, but not allowed to do so by the iron will of this frail and yet at the same time thick-set, quiet and gloomy man* with broad shoulders. (emphasis added) (Frank, *Mantle of the Prophet*, 39–40)

Dostoevsky himself, writing of gambling, says success is assured "if one is as though made of marble, cold, and *inhumanly* cautious." (Frank, *Miraculous Years*, 196)

To reaffirm his loyalty to the Russia he loved, from which he had endured so much grief, it is as if he had to demonstrate to himself that the constraint it offered actually was love, and the obedience it demanded really was necessary. To do that it had to be clear to him that he, in fact, needed the restraint that was the very nature of Russian life. How better to demonstrate that need than to show himself using freedom and rational method (the gambler's deluded faith in a "system") in the service only of his own destruction. He could choose discipline and obedient compliance over freedom by demonstrating—as he did with his mad gambling—that he was unworthy of freedom, showing, at the same time, Man's essentially guilty and sin-prone nature. By gambling, too, Dostoevsky continually repeated the emotional trauma of complete abandonment, and forever revived an impossible wish that the reality of captivity would suddenly change.

Between 1862 and 1864 Dostoevsky traveled twice in Europe. Not only did he gamble. He visited the major cities and saw the great cultural events. In London he visited the exhibit of the Crystal Palace. The Crystal Palace was a great glass and steel structure dedicated to introducing and promoting the glorious possibilities technology and industrial design offered for the improvement of Mankind. The significance of the exhibit and, for Dostoevsky, its atheistic implications figure fundamentally in *Notes from Underground*, written in 1865. In London, Dostoevsky also met the great Russian exile, the writer, editor, critic, and socialist, Alexander Herzen and the anarchist revolutionary, Michael Bakunin. He published an account of his first trip in *Winter Notes on Summer Impressions* in *Time* when he returned to Russia in 1863. In May of that year, by imperial order, the magazine was shut down.

In January 1863, there was an unsuccessful revolt in Poland against

Russian domination. Russian radicals could hardly voice their support for Poland. But Dostoevsky was not a radical. He deeply supported Russia against the Poles, and so did *Time*. But the magazine was shut down because of a piece that Nikolay Strakhov, a regular contributor to the journal and a friend of Dostoevsky, wrote. Although supporting Russia, Strakhov had argued, as Dostoevsky explained the case in a letter to the great Russian novelist and dramatist, Turgenev, that

> the Poles despise us as barbarians to such a degree, are so boastful to us of their "European" civilization, that one can scarcely foresee for a long time any moral peace (the only durable kind) with us. But as the exposition of the article was not understood, it was interpreted as follows: that we affirmed, *of ourselves*, that the Poles have a civilization so superior to ours, and we are so inferior, that obviously they are right and we are wrong. (*Stir of Liberation*, 211)

The staff of the magazine did not believe that the misunderstanding on the part of the government would persist. Mikhail and Dostoevsky believed that after explanations *Time* would be allowed to publish again, but such was not the case, and Mikhail set about trying to establish a new magazine and get license to publish it. He finally did succeed, and in March 1864, *Epokha (Epoch)* began publication.

During this period, Dostoevsky's domestic life was quite wretched. Marya was tubercular, reclusive, and tyrannical. The best picture of their relationship comes to us from the journal of Dostoevsky's second wife. Unlike Marya, she was attentive, loving and, indeed, saintly in her capacity to bear Dostoevsky's difficult character and destructive behavior:

> Really I was beside myself. That's all the thanks I get for never grumbling at him. It isn't worth controlling oneself. Marya Dimitrievna [Dostoevsky's first wife] never hesitated to call him a rogue and a rascal and a criminal, and to her he was like an obedient dog. (*Stir of Liberation*, 252, note)

During this period, too, Dostoevsky suffered badly from his epileptic attacks. To consult specialists, to get away from his domestic misery, to go back to the gaming tables and roulette, Dostoevsky decided to take another trip to Europe. He was also planning to meet Apollinaria Suslova in Paris. One of the ways he handled his domestic wretchedness was by falling in love with other women and seeking that they return his love.

Suslova was 21 in 1861, when she submitted *For the Time Being* to *Time*. It was published in October of that year. It was a story with the new feminist outlook which was developing then: a young woman runs away from a husband she did not love, ekes out a poor living on her own, dies of tuberculosis, but is triumphant in having asserted her independence and stayed true to herself. Suslova's sister was the first Russian woman to earn a medical degree. Dostoevsky and Suslova are thought to have become lovers during the winter of 1860. Soon, however, Suslova broke off the relationship. Her second husband, twenty years later in a letter to a friend reported this conversation he had with Suslova when he asked her why she left Dostoevsky:

> "Because he did not wish to divorce his wife, who was tubercular and dying.... She died six month later. But I was no longer in love with Feodor."
> "Why did you stop loving him?"
> "Because he would not get a divorce.... I gave myself to him, out of love, without asking anything. He should have behaved in the same way! He behaved otherwise and I left him. (*Stir of Liberation*)

Besides giving a sense of her relationship with Dostoevsky, Suslova reveals a governing and permanent aspect of his character, the conflict between duty and desire.

Dostoevsky left for Europe in August 1863 and returned in October. Before going to join Suslova in Paris, he stopped off at Wiesbaden to gamble. He won a considerable amount, lost half of it, and went on to Paris. His obsession with gambling lasted through the 1860s whenever he was in Europe. Relations with Suslova were perilous and painful. She had fallen for a Spaniard she met in the Latin Quarter and been jilted by him by the time Dostoevsky reached Paris. Dostoevsky and Suslova traveled through Italy and Germany together, separating in one city and meeting up in another. She was alternately affectionate and distant to Dostoevsky, putting him off but offering suggestions that they might become lovers again (they didn't); she tormented him sadistically. (*Stir of Liberation*, 269–275) In Wiesbaden, toward the end of the trip, Dostoevsky was gambling heavily and heavily impoverished. He met Turgenev there. Although they had had a falling out in the 1840s after Dostoevsky's first fame, when few could tolerate his combined arrogance and insecurity, they got on well. Dostoevsky borrowed money from him, which he paid back in 1875. Both Dostoevsky's experiences, as a vexed lover and as a driven roulette player, became the basis for *The Gambler* in 1866. But he would not start writing that until after he had written two of his best known works, *Notes from Underground* and *Crime and Punishment.*

During the time that *Epokha* was being published, perhaps the most important literary-political event in Russia was the publication of *What Is to Be Done?* a novel by Nikolai Chernyshevsky, Dostoevsky's ideological enemy who preached through his story a utilitarian-socialist-atheistic-materialism. Essentially he was one of a new movement of young people in Russia called "Nihilists." The Nihilists believed that there was nothing about the prevailing tsarist order that was sacred, and they were devoted to a violent revolution in the cause of a scientific and

Dostoevsky returned to St. Petersburg in October, and in January of the new year, Mikhail was given permission to start *Epokha.* The first issue appeared on March 21. It featured the first part of *Notes from Underground*, Dostoevsky's bitterly ironic refutation of spiritless materialism, human perfectibility, and the deification of mankind. Not a month later, on April 15, Dostoevsky's first wife succumbed to tuberculosis, leaving Dostoevsky to care for her son Pasha and leaving him also with the grief of her awful death and of their imperfect and troubled love. Not three months after her death, Dostoevsky's beloved brother and his partner in many of their life enterprises, Mikhail, died in his mid-forties, leaving a family. Besides his overwhelming grief, Dostoevsky also took upon himself responsibility for Mikhail's family and for Mikhail's debts. Mikhail's wife was not particularly well disposed to Dostoevsky and jealously resented any money spent on himself or on the family he later would have. Dostoevsky was angered by her lack of gratitude for the sacrifices he made for her family's sake, even to the point of pawning his and his wife's coats so that she might be able to keep hers. Burdensome as the obligation was, however, and thankless, he never shirked it.

humanist utopia. Their thinking showed the same sort of egotism, it seemed to Dostoevsky, as that which he found abhorrent in the partisans of the advancement suggested by the Crystal Palace. In Dostoevsky's view, both attitudes were founded on a vision of the individual free of the constraints of faith in God or belief in a world beyond this one. Both attitudes allowed the belief that individuals may act as they choose rather than as they must, as dictated by obedience to God. (*Stir of Liberation*, 371–4) Both believed in rationality. Dostoevsky had no faith in the power of rationality to extirpate the essential evil, which, he believed, defines humanity. For the Nihilists, the accepted use of violence in a revolutionary cause showed the hubris their denial of God permitted. The belief that people exist independently of God and are, therefore, free to act however they determine is the theme which Dostoevsky set out to illustrate and to challenge in *Crime and Punishment*.

The first mention Dostoevsky made of *Crime and Punishment* was in a letter he wrote from Wiesbaden where he was living in poverty in a hotel which would not serve him meals or even supply him with candles at night because he hadn't paid his bill. The letter was to Baron Wrangel asking for a loan of one hundred thalers. He also wrote to Alexander Milyukov about his proposed work and asked him to see if he could get a commission for it from a St. Petersburg journal. Milyukov was unable to, in part because Dostoevsky's attacks on Chernyshevsky rankled radicals. It was the anti-radical editor of the *Russian Messenger*, M.N. Katkov, who did publish it and began a long association with Dostoevsky. *Crime and Punishment* was a sensation. Years later Nikolay Strakhov remembered "[o]nly *Crime and Punishment* was read during 1866." (*Stir of Liberation*, 45) It brought more than five hundred new subscribers to the *Russian Messenger*. Dostoevsky was, nevertheless, being paid poorly. Moreover, because the story under his hand was growing longer than he had first thought, Katkov tried to lower the rate per page. The battle between them continued until Dostoevsky made a trip to Moscow and Katkov gave him a thousand-ruble advance. That was hardly enough and he continued to live in painful poverty.

Crime and Punishment became even more sensational because of two extra-literary events which occurred soon after its publication. In the first case, a student named Danilov killed a money lender and his servant, repeating in life Raskolnikov's crime in the novel. The second event had far greater political consequences. On April 4, 1866, a poor former student fired a shot at the tsar as he was stepping into his carriage in the Summer Gardens of the Winter Palace. A tradesman standing next to the student saw what was happening, jostled the student's arm just as he was firing the pistol, and thereby saved Alexander's life. Dostoevsky was thrown into frenzy by the news of the attempted assassination. Horror at the act was mingled with a dread of the political repression, which did, in fact, follow. Despite his fierce Russian patriotism and fervent love of the tsar, and despite his hatred for the atheistic Socialism embedded in Nihilism, Dostoevsky defended both freedom of speech:

> ... everybody now awaits with fear more constraints on speech and thought. They expect administrative controls. But how can nihilism be fought without freedom of speech? Even if they, the nihilists, were given freedom of speech, even then it would be more advantageous; they would make all Russia laugh by the *positive* explanation of their teachings.... [N]ow they are given the appearance of sphinxes, an enigma, wisdom, secrecy, and this fascinates the unexperienced. (*Miraculous Years*, 53)

and the students devoted to Nihilism:

> ... among us Russians ... we still have our own, eternally present *basic* point on which Socialism will long continue to be founded, that is [the] enthusiasm [of the young] for the good and their purity of heart.... [A]ll those high school pupils, those students, of whom I have seen so many, have become nihilists so purely, so unselfishly, in the name of honor, truth, and genuine usefulness. (*Miraculous Years*, 51)

Literary success and a place in the center of debate on the fundamental issues of the day did not however mean an easing of Dostoevsky's poverty, nor did it mean he was in a comfortable position in the market with regard to publishers. In fact Dostoevsky was laboring under a particularly unfavorable contract. Desperately in need of money, in 1865—he was in debt for three thousand rubles—Dostoevsky contracted with a particularly crafty and stingy publisher. He agreed to give Stellovsky, the publisher, the rights to publish a collection of his complete works for three thousand rubles and to give him, in addition, a new novel by November 1, 1866. Under the terms of their agreement, if Dostoevsky failed to deliver the novel on time, Stellovsky would gain the right to publish all of Dostoevsky's future work without having to give him even a kopeck in royalties for nine years. This wasn't bad enough. Stellovsky had—Dostoevsky did not know this—bought Dostoevsky's debt cheaply from his creditors and the three thousand rubles went back to him (Stellovsky).

Before he had entirely completed *Crime and Punishment*, Dostoevsky had to begin the next novel in order get it in by the November 1 deadline or suffer the harsh consequences. The book would be *The Gambler*, but Dostoevsky, who always underestimated the time it would take him to finish a book, was desperate by the first of October, afraid it would be impossible to finish on time. The solution, suggested by his friend Milyukov, was to hire a stenographer to whom Dostoevsky would dictate the book. Reluctantly and skeptically, he agreed. Milyukov asked an acquaintance who taught shorthand to find a stenographer for Dostoevsky.

Anna Grigoryevna Snitkina was young, smart, strong, comely, a "new woman," independent, but with the kind of old values that Dostoevsky held. She kept refusing, for example, at their first meeting, the cigarettes Dostoevsky—who was a heavy smoker—kept offering, showing that, although independent, she was not corrupted. Anna was the best stenographer in her class. They set to work, awkwardly at first, but Dostoevsky's need to talk and Anna's skill in bringing him out, and her interest in the novel he was dictating, including her ability to discuss its characters and themes with him, soon put Dostoevsky at ease. The work went swiftly. That in itself gladdened Dostoevsky's heart, but so did Anna's very presence, and the novel was ready on November 1. Stellovsky, true to his nature, was out of town that day and could not, therefore, receive it. He also had ordered his chief clerk to refuse it. If the novel did not get delivered, Dostoevsky would be in forfeit of all his work to Stellovsky. He and Anna had feared this, and she had had her mother consult with a lawyer. What Dostoevsky, therefore, was prepared to do in the event which actually transpired was to give the manuscript to the officer at the local police station near Stellovsky's and get a receipt. With Anna's help, he not only wrote *The Gamblers* in 26 days but also freed himself from Stellovsky's snare.

On November 8, 1866, Anna returned to Dostoevsky's flat to take his dictation of the last part of *Crime and Punishment*, but Dostoevsky began telling her about a dream he had of finding a small diamond. Then he told her a possible plot for a novel and said he wanted her help. After laying out the problem, he asked Anna to, "imagine ... that I have confessed my love to you and asked you to be my wife. Tell me, what would you answer?" Anna Grigoryevna wrote in her memoirs shortly before her death in 1918 that she "looked at his troubled face, which had become so dear to me, and said, 'I would answer that I love you and will love you all my life.'" (Dostoevsky, A., 46) They were married February 15, 1867. Anna did not marry Dostoevsky ignorant of his character, his gambling obsession, his illness, or his terrible debts. Despite the hostility of his brother Mikhail's widow and his stepson toward his new wife—they feared that her presence would hinder Dostoevsky's ability to support them, which he nevertheless continued to do throughout his life—Anna assumed the household management with his blessing. On April 14, however, they left Russia for Europe. It was supposed to be for three months, but the fear of being thrown into debtors' prison by his creditors kept Dostoevsky and his family abroad for four years. During that time, two daughters, Sonya and Lyubov were born to them. Sonya, died three months after birth.

Dostoevsky and Anna passed through Berlin and settled in three rooms in Dresden, where Dostoevsky hoped to begin writing his next book, but distractions were numerous. His epilepsy was milder, but he still suffered painful and unnerving episodes. He was, consequently even more irritable, quarrelsome, and (as Anna describes it in the shorthand diary she kept the first 18 months of the sojourn in Europe) "volcanic." Dostoevsky and Anna fought continually. Financially they were badly off, too, especially because Dostoevsky spent 10 days at the roulette tables of Hamburg a month after their arrival in Germany. And when he saw Turgenyev in Baden-Baden he fought with him because Turgenyev distanced himself from Russia and Russian nationalism so much as to declare that he now thought of himself as German, not Russian. The idea disgusted Dostoevsky, a passionate Russian nationalist. Dostoevsky and Anna did not settle long in one place but stopped in Geneva, went on to Vevey after a while, then to Milan, then Florence, then Prague, and finally back to Dresden in 1869. Their traveling could hardly have been comfortable even had they journeyed first class, but they traveled as cheaply as they could and rented poor rooms. All these distractions, however, were not fatal, for Dostoevsky began working on *The Idiot*, and in 1868 it was published in *Russian Messenger* in installments. In 1870, *The Eternal Husband* was published in *Dawn*.

Dostoevsky spent many hours each day in cafés reading the Russian newspapers. It was painful for him to stay out of Russia, but he would be imprisoned for debt if he returned. His poverty, too, was the rationale behind his feverish gambling. He stayed in touch with Russian politics and was as deeply involved with the intellectual currents which shaped political stances and actions as ever. He wrote *The Idiot* in part to counter the atheistic brutality, as he saw it, inherent in Nihilism with the spiritual beauty of the Christ-like suffering of Prince Myshkin. He wrote *The Devils*, which he began in his exile, to satirize Nihilist revolutionaries and to expose among the worst of them the cunning of their minds and the brutality of their souls. Excitement was added to the novel by the fact that a sensational trial involving murder among a group of young radicals was going on and Dostoevsky was drawing from it as he wrote the episodes, for the novel was serialized before being published in its full form. With *The Devils* the shift in Dostoevsky's politics became public knowledge. The political activist, Socialist, and prisoner-for-his-convictions had become a conservative, opposed to revolutionists with utopian ideals, and he portrayed them as criminal machiavells. Dostoevsky's return to Russia at just that time, in 1871, was not, however, supposed to be public knowledge because of his fear of debtors' prison. Only a few relatives and the publisher of *Russian World*, in which *The Devils* was being serialized, knew of his return.

Eight days after their return, Anna gave birth to a second son, whom they named Alyosha. He would live only three years. Dostoevsky secured payment from his Moscow publisher for past chapters and was able to move the family to a better apartment. He also wrote to the Tsarevitch, who would become Nicholas II, and he granted Dostoevsky a sum of money. Soon after giving birth Anna, who had convinced a tradesman to sell her furniture on installments before her delivery, now negotiated similarly with Dostoevsky's ferocious creditors. She explained to them that if they carried out their threats to send him to debtors' prison, Dostoevsky would be unable to earn any money to repay them and they, the creditors, would also incur his incarceration fees. If they permitted him to remain a free man, however, she could draw up a schedule of payments. They agreed, and Dostoevsky avoided prison. But he would yet go to prison once more, for two days, for a technical infraction of the censorship laws. He was treated well and allowed visitors.

In 1873, Dostoevsky became editor of *The Citizen*, a conservative journal owned by Dostoevsky's friend Prince Meshchersky, a friend, too, of Alexander. Thus Dostoevsky's conservative identification was well established. So it seemed odd when his next novel was serialized in *Notes of the Fatherland*, a liberal magazine run by his old political ally Nekrasov. *A Raw Youth*, the novel he wrote for Nekrasov is considered the weakest of his last five, and Dostoevsky complained that was because he felt constrained to write without violating the magazine's ideological parameters, which were not his. He also, it appears, used *A Raw Youth* to draw a philosophical picture of a world based on a vision—atheist, rationalist, and materialist—opposite to his own. It may be noted, too, that Dostoevsky did not feel the same stifling constraint from tsarist censors. He was irritated and hindered by the mechanics of the censorship, the rigmarole of the procedures, not by the fact of the censorship.

The years of the 1870s until his death in 1881 were exceptionally busy and productive ones. After resigning his post as editor of *The Citizen* in 1874, Dostoevsky began *A Raw Youth* and, in 1876 began publishing *The Diary of a Writer*. While he had edited *The Citizen*, Dostoevsky had written a column called "The Diary of a Writer." When he started an independent journal of that name, his idea was to write the entire thing himself, which he did. It was this two-year venture, not his novels, read primarily by the intelligentsia, which made Dostoevsky known and revered throughout all of Russia. During this period, too, Dostoevsky continued to suffer epileptic attacks, but, in addition, he came down with emphysema, a swelling of lung tissue. For treatment, he made several grueling trips to Bad Ems, a health spa in Germany, to drink the water there and rest. The waters seemed to do Dostoevsky some short-term good, but in a few years he did die of lung disease.

In *The Diary of a Writer*, Dostoevsky, by writing directly to the reader, established the kind of intimate rapport with his audience that he had not as a novelist, as esteemed and even as loved as he was as a novelist. He commented on the issues of the day, received many letters from readers about what he wrote, and even found strangers who had read his journal showing up at his doorstep. He usually brought them into his flat and spoke with them. It was also in *The Diary* that he gave vent to his deeply held anti-Semitism. Despite his strong devotion to Christian love, Dostoevsky was fiercely and obsessively anti-Semitic in his last years. He blamed the economic woes which the peasants faced after the liberation on "the Jews," whom he saw not only as a group apart from the Orthodox Christian Russians, but as a group opposed. But his anti-Semitism went against Dostoevsky's profound compassion for the suffering of mankind, and he suffered a split in his attitude. On the one hand he employed the familiar anti-Semitic stereotypes, including the ancient blood libel, that Jews kill Christian babies to use their blood for wine. On the other, he could present a sketch in his *Diary* imagining "the absolute stinking misery of a poor Jewish hut," in a freezing climate, in which a child has just been born. He then imagined a Christian doctor, "a righteous old man," who "has taken off his own wretched, worn uniform coat, has taken off his own shirt, and is tearing it up to make swaddling clothes." Dostoevsky called this act,

> the solution to the Jewish problem," and added, "Christ sees all this on high, and the doctor knows it: "This poor little Yid [Jew] will grow up and, perhaps, he himself may take the shirt from his back and give it to a Christian when he recalls the story of his birth" thinks the old man to himself with noble and naïve faith. Will this come to pass? Most likely it will not, yet it could come to pass: and on earth we can do nothing finer than to believe that this *can* and *will* come to pass. (*Mantle of the Prophet*, 317–318)

Besides offering a sentimentalized version of what can still be seen as an anti-Semitic attitude, this sketch also demonstrates a characteristic of Dostoevsky's worldview. It is one founded on the struggle between opposites not only of good and evil but of alienation and reconciliation. These are polarities which have played a defining role in his life, especially given his Siberian punishment, and in the formation of his personality, which had, consequently, to encompass despair and ecstasy.

His last work, *The Brothers Karamazov*, is an encyclopedia of the problems that confronted Dostoevsky in this polar fashion throughout his life and his work. Essentially, in *The Brothers Karamazov*, Dostoevsky explores the mystical, anti-rational transcendental response to the fundamental problems confronting mankind in life and the metaphysical quandaries plaguing us about death. By the time he began to write *The Brothers Karamazov*, Dostoevsky had become, in Joseph Frank's words, "a cult figure." (*Mantle of the Prophet*, 362) The clamor against it was intense when he suspended *The Diary*, even though he explained it was for matters of health and to begin a novel "which imperceptibly and involuntarily has been taking shape within me during the two years of the publication of the *Diary*. (*Mantle of the Prophet*, 361) He was also invited to an international congress of the Society of French Writers in Paris over which the literary hero of his youth, Victor Hugo, was presiding. But his health prevented him from attending.

Dostoevsky's last year was as eventful politically as any of his life. He had been selected on February 2, 1880 by the members of the Slavic Benevolent Society to write a tribute to be presented to Alexander II on February 19 in honor of his 25 year on the Russian Imperial throne. On the evening of February 5 a bomb exploded just under the dining room of the Winter Palace. The tsar and his guests were not hurt, but many soldiers and others were either killed or injured. The blast was set by a member of the revolutionary group, the People's Will, a cabinet maker who worked in the palace and had slowly smuggled in the bomb parts. Martial law was imposed. Dostoevsky supported it, but in his tribute to the tsar, when he referred to the attack, rather than denouncing the group responsible for the bombing, he blamed "the cultured stratum of society" for "not believing in either the Russian people or its truth, nor even in God." The revolutionaries themselves, he describes as "the young Russian energies, alas, so sincerely deluding themselves," who "have at last fallen under the power of dark, underground forces." (*Mantle of the Prophet*, 478–481) The model of good being undermined by evil still existed for him, as did his idea of the inherent goodness of the Russian people and the corrupting influence of European intellectualism.

Dostoevsky's last public appearance was on June 8, 1880, when he spoke at the Pushkin festival held in Moscow to honor the great poet at the unveiling of a monument to him. Turgenyev spoke on June 7, hailing Pushkin as "the first Russian artist-poet," (*Mantle of the Prophet*, 515) as opposed to a folk poet. Dostoevsky, the next day drew a picture of Pushkin as a representative of the Russian people, their mystical faith, and their connection to the soil. His speech was greeted with tumultuous acclaim.

Dostoevsky died seven months later on January 28, 1881. Just a few days earlier, he was accepting an invitation to the Winter Palace. He was receiving visits from two of his oldest friends, Apollon Maikov and Nikolay Strakov. He was planning to participate in a Pushkin evening. He went to the printing plant to oversee production of the next issue of *The Diary*, which he had resumed. At dinner that evening, he and Anna spoke about Mr. Pickwick, whom Dostoevsky had always taken as a comic representation of Christ, and he had always revered Dickens. He left the table and wrote a letter to N.A. Lyubimov, his editor at the *Russian Messenger,* typically asking to be paid for the last chapters of *Karamazov*. He was planning to buy a country estate for his family.

His death began the night of January 25 with a nosebleed, which was the result apparently of his bending down and moving a heavy piece of furniture to retrieve a pen which had fallen off his night table. The bleeding stopped immediately. He mentioned it to Anna, but paid no further attention to it. It worried Anna, however. She called the doctor, but he was delayed in coming. That afternoon, Dostoevsky had engaged in a typical, for him, strenuous argument with a visiting friend who was also fond of arguing. Anna tried to keep the friends calm. Later that afternoon, before dinner, Dostoevsky collapsed on his couch and Anna was horrified to see his chin covered with blood and blood streaming into his beard. Dostoevsky was confined to bed, took last rites, and died with Anna and their children at his bedside after he fell into a coma.

When Dostoevsky's death was announced in the newspapers, Anna wrote in her memoir,

> Known and unknown [visitors] arrived to pray at his coffin, and there were so many that very quickly all the five rooms were filled with a dense crowd, and when the office for the dead was recited the children and I had a hard time pushing through the crowd to stand near the coffin. (*Mantle of the Prophet*, 750)

The head of censorship, N.S. Abaza presented Anna with a letter from the Ministry of Finance announcing that the Tsar Alexander II had ordered that she be given a pension for life of 2,000 rubles a year "because of [Dostoevsky's] services to Russian literature. Dostoevsky's funeral procession through St. Petersburg stretched for nearly a mile.

The crowd that came out for it was estimated at 30,000. He was buried at the cemetery of the Alexander Nevsky Monastery.

WORKS CITED

Dostoevsky, Anna. *Dostoevsky: Reminiscences*, Beatrice Stillman, ed. and trans. New York: Liveright, 1975, 448 p.

Frank, Joseph. *Dostoevsky: The Seeds of Revolt, 1821–1849*. Princeton: Princeton University Press, 1976, 401 p.

———. *Dostoevsky: The Years of Ordeal, 1850–1859*. Princeton: Princeton University Press, 1983, 320 p.

———. *Dostoevsky: The Stir of Liberation, 1860–1865*. Princeton: Princeton University Press, 1986, 395 p.

———. *Dostoevsky: The Miraculous Years, 1865–1871*. Princeton: Princeton University Press, 1995, 523 p.

———. *Dostoevsky: The Mantle of the Prophet, 1871–1881*. Princeton: Princeton University Press, 2002, 784 p.

———. and David I. Goldstein. *Selected Letters of Fyodor Dostoyevsky*, Andrew R. MacAndrew, trans. New Brunswick and London: Rutgers University Press, 1987, 543 p.

Goldstein, David I. *Dostoyevsky and the Jews*. Austin and London: University of Texas Press, 1981, 231 p.

Grossman, Leonid. *Dostoevsky: His Life and Work*, Mary Mackler, trans. Indianapolis/New York: The Bobbs-Merrill Company, Inc., 1975, 647 p.

Kjetsaa, Geir. *Fyodor Dostoevsky: A Writer's Life*, Siri Hustvedt and David McDuff, trans. New York: Elizabeth Sifton Books/Viking, 1987, 437 p.

Mochulsky, Konstantin. *Dostoevsky: His Life and Work*, Michael A. Minihan, trans. Princeton: Princeton University Press, 1967, 687 p.

Sekirin, Peter. *The Dostoevsky Archive: Firsthand Accounts of the Novelist from Contemporaries' Memoirs and Rare Periodicals, with a Detailed Lifetime Chronology and Annotated Bibliography*. Jefferson, North Carolina, and London: McFarland & Company, Inc. Publishers, 1997, 370 p.

Yarmolinsky, Avraham. *Dostoevsky: Works and Days*. New York: Funk & Wagnalls, 1971, 438 p.

http://www.kiosek.com/dostoevsky/critical_works.html

http://www.uoregon.edu/~kimball/Petrashevtsy.htm

RACHEL THOMAS

Ideas Imbued and the Exploration of Experience: The Works of Fyodor Dostoevsky

"He is one of those who don't need millions, they just need to get an idea straight."

-Alyosha, *The Brothers Karamazov*

INTRODUCTION

Fyodor Dostoevsky was, above all else, an explorer of ideas. His passion for ideological exploration led him to intellectual pursuits, a journalistic livelihood, and the creation of literary masterpieces. As recounted in the preceding biography, Dostoevsky's life coincided with a particularly tumultuous period in Russian history, and was undoubtedly shaped by the sociopolitical happenings he witnessed. His intellectual and literary growth progressed alongside Russian society's larger experimentation with radical "isms"—anarchism, atheism, even feminism—and the lens through which Dostoevsky perceived his life experiences was shaded by the movements that colored news of the day.

Themes, settings, and characters found in his works will seem familiar to readers who have studied Dostoevsky's life. Characters that brighten his pages, and the pursuits with which they busy themselves, are reminiscent of Dostoevsky's own experience with the intellectual circles, social structures, and spiritual communities of mid-nineteenth century Russia.

Alongside representations of historical events in his books, reflections of Dostoevsky's personal life also proliferate in terms no less obvious: allusions to his struggle with epilepsy, experiences with death, and his strong spirituality are unmistakable. With such clear parallels between the life and times of the author and those incidents and settings found in his novels, it is not surprising that the reader might, at first glance, understand Dostoevsky's works as at least partially autobiographical. Great minds have found segments of the author's life inlaid in his novels and comprehended those works as literal expressions of his personal views. Understanding the relationship of the author to his work is, indeed, a daunting task, and we must begin by examining the literary form Dostoevsky chose to express his stories and the ideas they carry.

LITERARY STRUCTURE: AN EXPERIENCE OF IDEAS

It has been said that, with regard to form, the works of Fyodor Dostoevsky constitute very bad literature. Victor Terras noted, "If the ideal is a well-spaced and economically developed linear plot, a Dostoevskian novel with its multitude of minor characters and subplots, inserted anecdotes, philosophical dialogues, and the narrator's essayistic and other digressions is hardly 'well structured'." (4)

The author's note to *The Brothers Karamazov* exemplifies the convoluted style to which Terras points. Though it is seemingly delivered by the storyteller, it features a voice separate from that of the narrator. It is presented as a note of explanation for the story to come, but instead leaves the reader unclear as to what he is about to read, or what he should draw from the text: The speaker professes Alyosha as the hero but doubts his ability to prove himself as such; he also refers to a second, more important, volume that Dostoevsky never writes. This type of contradictory segment is repeated often in Dostoevsky's works, and this leads many to find his prose lacking in coherent messages. In fact, while one easily recognizes themes drawn from the author's life in each novel, it is impossible to characterize a single voice in any one of them as belonging to Dostoevsky.

Nearly all of Dostoevsky's major works have a polyphonic structure: one in which multiple voices and views are treated with equal weight. Even the monologic exception, *Notes from the Underground*, changes direction with such astounding speed and frequency that the reader who attempts to find a sentence containing Dostoevsky's "point" is as unsuccessful as one who peruses *The Brothers Karamazov*.

The Dostoevskian novel includes a group of character voices moving in different ideological directions, and presenting contradictory messages. Despite the fact that many of his works feature a prominent narrator, the reader's search for a unified message is hindered by the narrator's peripheral nature in his tale. Dostoevsky's narrators never seem sure that they have the story right—they are always aware of the alternate vantage points presented by the characters they describe.

Although a single, clearly articulated viewpoint is absent from each of Dostoevsky's novels, the skill with which he concocts his web of characters and ideas, subplots, and subtexts suggests that the resultant state of affairs—though quite mangled—is just what he set out to create. Dostoevsky tangles his stories precisely to keep the reader from plucking his "voice" whole from the pages of his works.

In examining the polyphonic structure of Dostoevsky's fiction, Terras notes that the author's works encompass not only multiple characters with contradictory statements, but often full philosophies and antagonistic value systems. (5) At points, Dostoevsky plays devil's advocate with every possible view on a question or issue. *The Brothers Karamazov* is, again, an appropriate example of this tendency, where four Karamazov sons espouse four contradictory—and often competing—philosophies on life.

In addition to endowing major characters with contradictory opinions, Dostoevsky also imbues relatively minor, even obscure characters with important statements, and sometimes lengthy diatribes. He trusts the weighty exploration of life after death to the cranky and consumptive Ippolit, whose only other use in *The Idiot* is to irk those around him with false threats and general discontent. In the same novel, the lazy, gambling widower Lebedev is chosen to introduce the theme of universal responsibility for individual sin—so well known from *The Brothers Karamazov*—in his prayer for the Comtesse du Barry. (*Idiot*, Pt. 2, Sec. 2) Even in *The Brothers Karamazov* itself, which centers on the question of why innocents must suffer, the all-important "innocent" is represented by the young consumptive son of a drunken captain, Ilyusha—a shadow of a youth whose role is completely eclipsed by that of his schoolmate, Kolya.

Presented with countless voices and conflicting opinions, one can easily wander astray in the search for Dostoevsky's intended message. Robert L. Belknap notes that even D.H. Lawrence misunderstood

Dostoevsky's purpose, deducing from his legend of the Grand Inquisitor that Dostoevsky found Jesus an inadequate role model for a righteous life. (53) Mikhail Bakhtin closely examines this issue of locating Dostoevsky's voice in his *Problems of Dostoevsky's Poetics*—an apt title for this complex journey to find Dostoevsky's viewpoint in his works. Bakhtin finds the reader's confusion directly related to the sheer number of voices in Dostoevsky's works—in the fact that his works are polyphonic rather than monologic.

In the monologic work, a single mode of thinking is clearly expressed—the author speaks through a single character, and the ideas he wants his audience to retain are expressed directly in the words of that figure. (Bakhtin, 68) The action of the work affirms this protagonist's truth. The ideas of other characters are negated and are therefore recognized as opposed to the author's beliefs. Dostoevsky's works are much less simplistic. His novels are polyphonic, and he was thus prevented from feeding his beliefs to the reader in such a direct fashion. (Bakhtin, 63)

To organize the polyphony in his works, Dostoevsky associates not only the characters' words, but also his actions with the ideas they carry. With each character delineating a separate viewpoint—and one that often competes with those of other figures—the image of the idea becomes inseparable from the image of the character. Each character becomes associated with a single idea or thought process, and his importance lies in that idea, rather than in his personality or action set. The figure ceases to be simply a personality acting in time; he becomes what Bakhtin refers to as a "carrier of ideas." (63) In this context, Rakitin is understood as the intellectual, representing the radical popular thought (i.e., atheism, Nihilism). Ippolit carries the idea, or question, of what follows death and how faith is or is not related to it.

Most of the "carriers of ideas" in Dostoevsky's novels are not negated—rejected—through the action of the work, as they would be in monologic works. Therefore, multiple "carriers of ideas"—many in direct conflict with one another—appear in a novel as valid and, in some way, important to the reader's literary experience. Again, the confusion over which idea might be "the one" Dostoevsky wants his audience to believe is natural.

It is precisely this compulsion to find one coherent message that must be discarded if the reader is to fully understand and appreciate

Dostoevsky's novels. While the reader has been wading through countless opinions and ideas expressed by various characters in search of the "truth" in a work, it turns out that Dostoevsky fashions a truth from the combination and interaction of those many ideas. Instead of picking one, his multiple "carriers of ideas" must be taken together as creating a larger thought process, a full consciousness that he seeks to convey to the reader. As Bakhtin explains the phenomena, the *unity of existence* in a monologic work—where one character's ideas constitute the full truth—is replaced in Dostoevsky's polyphonic novels with a *unity of consciousness.* (65). Dostoevsky does not lead his reader through a series of character statements to express a set of his views; he creates a reality for the reader to explore, a web of characters and ideas to experience. Having done so, he hopefully leads his audience to understand and appreciate beliefs that he has come to in the process of living, and writing his works. Bakhtin makes an important insight when he notes that Dostoevsky works "not in thoughts, but in points of view, in consciousnesses, in voices." (76)

This new view of Dostoevsky's poetics is further complicated by the realization that the ideas he associates with his characters are not usually simple ones. Rather, a single character often encompasses something much closer to a world view or a philosophy or life—what Dostoevsky called *Weltanschauung.* (*Letters*, 109) The consciousness woven for the audience through its introduction to many "carriers of ideas" is a highly complex one, with not only ideas, but developed world views competing and combining to create a larger awareness in each novel.

In short, when looking for the author's thoughts directly in the words of his characters, the reader will undoubtedly be disappointed. One must resist the temptation to single out any one of the many "carriers of ideas," instead embracing the novel mode of ideological expression developed in Dostoevsky's works.

William Mills Todd III did not see Dostoevsky as an underachiever in the category of literary structure. Rather, he understood the author as rejecting the traditional boundaries of the novelistic form—in his use of multiple voices, but also in the structures that his characters reject and the alternative ones Dostoevsky subsequently creates for them. Todd suggests that, in *The Brothers Karamazov*, Dostoevsky presents a set of poetics that his characters emphatically reject: "excessive narratorial distance, egocentric narratorial involvement, rigid master plots, formal rules." (Engelstein, 278)

These restrictive structures are replaced with a new set of "positive poetics" (Engelstein, 278), best displayed in the legend of the Grand Inquisitor. In a letter written to K.P. Pobedonostsev, Dostoevsky describes how he set out to answer the clear-cut statements of the Grand Inquisitor:

> ... The answer is not a direct one aimed at propositions which have already been stated point-by-point (in the Grand Inquisitor or earlier), but merely an oblique one. It will be something directly [and inversely] opposite to the *weltanschauung* which has been stated already, but again, it is presented not point-by-point, but, so to speak, in an artistic picture. (Bakhtin, 80)

As has been discussed, the polyphonic form he chose prevented Dostoevsky from presenting a clear ideology for his readers. Instead, he leads his audience through an experiential picture, aided by his "carriers of ideas" combined, that challenges one's most profoundly held beliefs about society and spirituality.

In the absence of familiar literary structures, Dostoevsky's characters seem incomplete, despite their association with a specific *Weltanschauung*. Though the thoughts expressed by these figures are complex and of great depth, intellectual moments often glimmer in otherwise dull and underdeveloped personas. In a very real sense, the development of his "carriers of ideas" is left unfinished: They are unbounded and, therefore, boundless. Returning for a moment to the authorial note of *The Brothers Karamazov*, one finds Dostoevsky admits to unfinished character and ideological development without apology:

> Being at a loss to resolve these questions, I am resolved to leave them without any resolution. To be sure, the keen-sighted reader will already have guessed long ago that that is what I've been getting at from the very beginning and will only be annoyed with me for wasting fruitless words and precious time. To this I have a ready answer: I have been wasting fruitless words and precious time, first, out of politeness, and, second, out of cunning. At least I have given some warning beforehand. (4)

He cannot answer the questions he raises, and so will not make the attempt. The ideas carried by his characters are open-ended, welcoming the reaction and influence of the audience as much as they succeed in influencing those readers.

Though the consciousness that Dostoevsky creates in his works is complex and multilayered, one might charge that the experience he offers the audience deals more often with the exceptional than with events and themes of daily life. It is an apt charge, and a habit that set Dostoevsky apart from many of his contemporaries—particularly Tolstoy, who painted scenes of "normal" Russian life.

Straying from the norm occasionally got Dostoevsky into trouble, when the society that served as his immediate audience misunderstood his writing and took his statements literally. In a letter to Doctor Alexander Fyodorovich Blagonravov in 1880, Dostoevsky wrote:

> Because of that chapter in the 'Karamazovs' (of the hallucination) with which you, as a physician, are so pleased, it has already been sought to stamp me as a reactionary and fanatic; who has come to believe in the Devil.... But I believe they will find themselves mistaken. (*Letters*, 259)

Rather seeking to laud devil-worship in the scene where Ivan communes with inner demons, Dostoevsky aimed to achieve the greatest level of accuracy in his portrayal of hallucinatory experience. The fact that he was subsequently branded a fanatic proves that the reason behind his realism was lost on these first readers.

Dostoevsky's concentration on exceptions to normal experience is tied to his personal idea of realism: he saw his development of accounts from society's edges as representing a larger truth. Writing to Nikolai Nikolaivich Strakhov in 1869, he noted that, "What most people regard as fantastic and lacking in universality, I hold to be the inmost essence of truth. Arid observation of everyday trivialities I have long ceased to regard as realism—it is quite the reverse." (*Letters*, 167) Terras notes that Dostoevsky understood the psychology of poverty, humiliation, resentment, jealousy, cynicism, and cruelty better than most (10). Thus, it was these abnormal states that he included in his novels, in order to achieve the greatest level of realism in his works.

Though Dostoevsky represented the extraordinary more

frequently and skillfully than the everyday, he drew details from factual sources. In an 1879 letter to his editor, discussing the basis for Ivan's views on the senseless suffering of children, he noted that "all the stories about children happened, were printed in the papers, and I can show where; nothing was invented by me ..." (Bloom, 54) W.J. Leatherbarrow shows him as a man obsessed by facts, a truth evident in this excerpt from his notebooks for *A Raw Youth*:

> "Facts. They pass before us. No one noticed them [...] I cannot tear myself away, and all the cries of the critics to the effect that I do not depict real life have not disenchanted me. There are no bases to our society [...] One colossal quake and the whole lot will come to an end, collapse and be negated as though it had never existed. And this is not just outwardly true, in the West, but inwardly, morally so. Our talented writers, people like Tolstoi and Goncharov, who with great artistry depict family life in upper-middle-class circle, think that they are depicting the life of the majority. In my view, they have depicted only the life of the exceptions, but the life which I portray is the life that is the general rule. Future generations, more objective in their view, will see that this is so. The truth is on my side, I am convinced of that."
> (Leatherbarrow, 4)

Dostoevsky's concentration on the fringes of society is further explained when one considers the larger consciousness that his multiple characters and ideas combine to create. No single figure or ideology is meant to be understood as containing the content of a full life. Rather, one should see that, through his "carriers," Dostoevsky represented ideas one might find in the context of a larger life experience.

Typical individuals exist only on the fringe of Dostoevsky's novels, and the accepted "normal" parts of life, such as happy marriage, also abide in those outer realms. (Terras, 37) This is so because Dostoevsky explores specific queries and subjects in each of his novels, and thus creates literary experiences specific to those questions and themes. There is much less to examine in the acceptable center of society than at the less understood and less commonly lived fringes.

Exploring Lived Experience

As Harold Bloom notes in the introduction to this volume, "that the writer somehow is in the work, we need not doubt." The search to find the author may be highly complex, though, as is the case with Dostoevsky. It is equally important, however, to find the work in the author: to understand how Dostoevsky was affected by his surroundings, his life, and literary experiences, and how those were translated back into his writing. In his examination of the themes of Dostoevskian novels, Leatherbarrow seeks:

> to foreground the fact that Dostoevsky's writings were produced amidst a variety of cultural stimuli and assumptions, and to encourage awareness of the extent to which the nature of his texts was subject to manipulation—sometimes in ways acknowledged explicitly, on other occasions implicitly—by the effects of those cultural stimuli and of the societal structures and relationships in which the process of production was embedded." (10–11)

Such an inquiry into the context of Dostoevsky's works gives one not only an understanding of the author's motivations, but also the way those motivations play out in his prose.

When examining the influences that shaped Dostoevsky's style, one should not overlook the effect of serialization on the format and tone of his works. (Leatherbarrow 10–11) Many of Dostoevsky's novels were serialized in the journals of his day, giving him opportunities for feedback during the writing process, but also creating a direct link between income and literature in his life. In many senses, he was restricted by the censorship requirements in place when each work was written. (Leatherbarrow, 13) Further, the fact of serialization highlights the extent to which Dostoevsky was at the mercy of his audience: Social trends affected his popularity and readership and likely influenced his choice of literary subjects.

In addition to unavoidable cultural influences, a number of potent themes from Dostoevsky's own life found their way into his works repeatedly, in ways that cannot be mistaken for coincidental overlap between life and art.

Dostoevsky suffered from increasingly frequent epileptic fits throughout his adult life, and his illness is mirrored in the epilepsy of two major characters. In *The Brothers Karamazov*, the Karamazov half-brother, Smerdyakov, suffers from epilepsy and uses his illness as a false alibi for committing patricide.

The title character of *The Idiot*, Prince Lev Myshkin, is a second epileptic who experiences two fits during the course of the novel. Both of these are described with a level of detail unquestionably made possible by Dostoevsky's experience with similar bouts of illness. Baron Alexander Wrangel, a close friend, gave the following account of Dostoevsky's illness:

> And now I must relate what I know of his epileptic fits. I never, thank God, saw one of them. But I know that they frequently recurred; his landlady usually sent for me at once. After the fits he always felt shattered for two or three days, and his brain would not work. The first fits, as he declared, had overtaken him in Petersburg; but the malady had developed in prison. At Semipalatinsk he would have one every three months. He told me that he could always feel the fit coming on, and always experienced beforehand an indescribable sense of well-being. After each attack he presented a woe-fully dejected aspect. (*Letters*, 299–300)

A similar description of "indescribable sense of well-being" in the account of Myshkin's fit shows not only the way that Dostoevsky explored incidents from his life in his works, but also the degree to which he drew from his personal understanding of epilepsy to ensure the realism of his characters:

> He remembered that during his epileptic fits, or rather immediately preceding them, he had always experienced a moment or two when his whole heart, and mind, and body seemed to wake up to vigour and light; when he became filled with joy and hope, and all his anxieties seemed to be swept away for ever; these moments were but presentiments, as it were, of the one final second (it was never more than a second) in which the fit came upon him. That second, of

course, was inexpressible. When his attack was over, and the prince reflected on his symptoms, he used to say to himself: "These moments, short as they are, when I feel such extreme consciousness of myself, and consequently more of life than at other times, are due only to the disease—to the sudden rupture of normal conditions. Therefore they are not really a higher kind of life, but a lower." (*The Idiot*, Pt. 2, Ch. 5)

That Dostoevsky was curious about his illness is evident from the way he explored epilepsy in his works. It is particularly interesting to note the range of personality and societal situation encompassed by his two epileptic characters—one a nearly Christ-like figure, one a bastard parricide—particularly given the seeming relation between epileptic fits and the spirituality of the afflicted characters.

His multiple experiences with death no doubt informed representations of natural death and murder in Dostoevsky's works. He lost his mother at the age of 16 and, only two years later, his father was murdered by the family's serfs. In a period of five years between 1864 and 1869, Dostoevsky lost his first wife, his brother Mikhail, and his infant daughter. (Leatherbarrow XIV) The loss of his mother provided him with experiential knowledge for the creation of multiple motherless characters, including Prince Myshkin, Sonya, Nastasya Fillipova, and Katerina Ivanovna. The theme of parricide is, of course, central to his crowning literary achievement, *The Brothers Karamazov*.

In 1849, for his involvement in the radical intellectual Petrashvetsy Circle, Dostoevsky was sentenced to death and subjected to a mock execution before receiving a pardon and a four-year sentence to hard labor in Siberia (Grossman). It is worthwhile to compare his personal recollection of this traumatic experience with thoughts on the subject of execution offered by Myshkin in *The Idiot*. On the day of his pardon, Dostoevsky sent a short letter to his brother Mikhail, recounting what he ostensibly took to be the most important details of the day:

> Today, the 22nd of December, we were all taken to Semyonovsky Square. There the death-sentence was read to us, we were given the Cross to kiss, the dagger was broken over our heads, and our funeral toilet (white shirts) was made. Then three of us were put standing before the

palisades for the execution of the death-sentence. I was sixth in the row; we were called up by groups of three, and so I was in the second group, and had not more than a minute to live. I thought of you, my brother, and of yours; in that last moment you alone were in my mind; then first I learnt how very much I love you, my beloved brother! I had time to embrace Plestcheiev and Dourov, who stood near me, and to take my leave of them. Finally, retreat was sounded, those who were bound to the palisades were brought back, and it was read to us that His Imperial Majesty granted us our lives. Then the final sentences were recited. Palm alone is fully pardoned. He has been transferred to the line with the same rank. F. Dostoevsky. (*Letters*, 53)

In Part I of *The Idiot*, during his first meeting with the Yepanchin women, Myshkin recounts his witness of an execution by guillotine, and his thoughts on the subject of death by execution:

A murder by sentence is far more dreadful than a murder committed by a criminal. The man who is attacked by robbers at night, in a dark wood, or anywhere, undoubtedly hopes and hopes that he may yet escape until the very moment of his death. There are plenty of instances of a man running away, or imploring for mercy—at all events hoping on in some degree—even after his throat was cut. But in the case of an execution, that last hope—having which it is so immeasurably less dreadful to die,—is taken away from the wretch and *certainty* substituted in its place! There is his sentence, and with it that terrible certainty that he cannot possibly escape death—which, I consider, must be the most dreadful anguish in the world. You may place a soldier before a cannon's mouth in battle, and fire upon him—and he will still hope. But read to that same soldier his death-sentence, and he will either go mad or burst into tears. Who dares to say that any man can suffer this without going mad? No, no! it is an abuse, a shame, it is unnecessary—why should such a thing exist? Doubtless there may be men who have been sentenced, who have suffered this mental anguish for a while and then have been reprieved; perhaps such men may have been able to relate their feelings afterwards. Our Lord Christ spoke of this anguish and dread. No! no! no! No man should be treated so, no man, no man! (*Idiot*, Pt. 1, Ch. 2)

Contrasting the factual account from Dostoevsky's letter to the much more emotional one in his novel highlights the relationship that the author cultivated between his real life and his works: Where life proved too painful for examination in reality, he retreated to the confines of his novels for exploration of his experiences.

Dostoevsky's experience in chains affected him greatly. With regard to his literature, it provided him with considerable background for his *Memoirs from the House of the Dead*, and gave him intimate knowledge of the logistical details for Dmitri Karamazov's journey to Siberia. More significantly, Dostoevsky's time in prison gave him an appreciation for the common people of Russia that is evident in his later works, particularly *The Brothers Karamazov*. In 1854, Dostoevsky wrote to his brother Mikhail, of his experience in Siberia, revealing his new-found conviction that

> ... Men everywhere are just—men. Even among the robber-murderers in the prison, I came to know some men in those four years. Believe me, there were among them deep, strong, and beautiful natures, and it often gave me great joy to find gold under a rough exterior. And not in a single case, or even two, but in several cases. Some inspired respect; others were downright fine. (*Letters*, 65)

This appreciation for the lower levels of Russian society was to remain with Dostoevsky throughout the rest of his days. His empathy for the lower classes, coupled with a sense of detachment gained from his time spent away from Russian society, affected his view of the intellectual and political movements that blossomed in the 1860s, a subject to be explored in the following section.

It is valid to ask why Dostoevsky included the subjects he did—so clearly drawn from his personal life—in his novels and writings. Several possibilities exist to explain the relationship between the author's life experiences and the themes of his works. It may have been that Dostoevsky knew these certain subjects—epilepsy, gambling, and others described herein—so well from his own life that he drew upon them simply to make his accounts more factual, to enhance his own type of realism. It is equally possible that Dostoevsky included these bits of lived experience in his works to explore and better understand his own life, his own self. Perhaps these personal details are included as much to aid in Dostoevsky's formation of personal opinions as to add realistic flair to his prose. In all likelihood, his motivation was a combination of both conjectures.

Regardless of the reason for their inclusion, one must recognize that, while there are many situations in his works drawn almost directly from Dostoevsky's own life, this is not the case universally. Notably, though his time spent imprisoned with murderers may have given him considerable insight into the mind of a killer, he manages to carry his reader very convincingly through Raskolnikov's thought processes without having committed murder himself. Dostoevsky included these themes—and indeed, exact incidents from his life—in order to enhance the realism of his novels and to better comprehend his own experiences. He did not, however, imbue his works with the feelings and opinions related to those personal events in a way that sways the reader particularly in favor of a particular viewpoint. Speeches that reveal his experience are thrown into the mix of competing thoughts and accounts. Ippolit's certainty that his own death from consumption is hopeless and horrible counters Myshkin's belief that execution is worse. In truth, Dostoevsky does not include opinions at all, only experiences and ideas for the reader to explore.

THE INTELLECTUAL AND THE RUSSIAN QUESTION

It is clear from the content of his novels that Dostoevsky was keenly aware of—and intimately affected by—the societal constructs and intellectual movements encircling him. His Siberian exile resulted from involvement with the more radical sectors of the Russian intellectual community in the 1840s, a decade of harsh governmental censorship and general suppression of scholarly circles. Despite these hindrances to an open intellectual life, Dostoevsky fell in with the Petrashevtsy Circle an affiliation that ultimately led to his imprisonment, death-sentence, mock execution, pardon, and alternative hard labor in Siberia.

One would hardly be surprised if Dostoevsky's experience with an anti-intellectual government permanently curbed his involvement in radical circles, or if it led him to steer clear of radical ideologies altogether. Yet, given his continued employment with intellectual journals following his return from Siberia, it is clear that Dostoevsky did not, in fact, shy away from the examination of timely political and social movements in the St. Petersburg to which he returned. Rather, he continued to include descriptions and examinations of many such dogmas in his later novels.

One should not deduce, however, that Dostoevsky was unchanged by his imprisonment, or his extended absence from St. Petersburg. He returned, in 1859, to a very different Russia than the one he left a decade earlier. A new and considerably more liberal tsar, Alexander II, had taken the throne, the serfs had subsequently been emancipated, and much of the censorship that had kept progressive political factions behind closed doors in the 1840s had been repealed. (Leatherbarrow, 15)

His 10-year hiatus from St. Petersburg afforded Dostoevsky a critical distance from which to view the social and political fervor of Alexander II's more open society: the ideologies of Nihilism, atheism, feminism, and socialism among others. While he did not fail to examine these concepts in his works, he was increasingly conservative in his personal views, becoming an ardent nationalist in his post-Siberian years. In part because of his new appreciation for the plight of the Russian common people, he came to favor a return to what he saw as traditional Russian values. In a letter to Apollon Nikolayevitch Maikov in 1856, before his return to St. Petersburg, Dostoevsky described his new nationalist leanings:

> I mean about patriotism, the Russian Idea, the sense of duty, national honour, and all those things of which you speak with such enthusiasm.... For I was always inspired by those very emotions and convictions.... I wholly share your patriotic emotion, your efforts toward the moral emancipation of the Slavs.... Yes—indeed I do share your idea that in Russia Europe will find her final account; it is Russia's true mission. (*Letters*, 85)

Having been absent during the 10 years in which socialism took root and atheism was announced, Dostoevsky had not witnessed the nature of their growth in Russia, but he recognized Western ideals in their philosophies. He saw Russia as a place where natural man was being corrupted by radical influence moving eastward, and there is an unmistakable tension in his portrayal of what he saw as Western pressures. He understood Russia as the chosen site for an ideological battle of sorts: the source from which traditional ideals would reemerge victorious in the face of Western modernization.

Dostoevsky, as he examined his rapidly changing homeland, understood the growth of radical intellectualism in the Russia of the 1860s as resulting from this Western intellectual influence. He associated the image of the intellectual who carried foreign ideals as a negative Western symbol. Thus, while he explored the tenets and theories of many radical ideologies in his novels, the obsessed intellectual characters that he imbued with Western ideas are ultimately—at the conclusion of his emblematic idea exploration—redeemed from, or destroyed by, their intellectualism.

Intellectuals are the central figures in several Dostoevskian novels: The action of *Crime and Punishment* trails the student and tutor Raskolnikov, as *Notes from the Underground* follows the disparate ranting of a philosophical misanthrope. While professing Alyosha as hero of *The Brothers Karamazov*, the author devotes a large number of his scenes to the description and exploration of Ivan's atheist conjectures. Amateur intellects of lesser importance—Rakitin and Kolya in *The Brothers Karamazov*, and Ippolit in *The Idiot*—crowd around the major minds and spout less fully developed philosophies as easily recognized from histories of mid-nineteenth century Russia. The words and actions of such intellectual personages—large and small—and their collective existence in each novel, allowed Dostoevsky to explore concepts of atheism, Nihilism, feminism, nationalism, for the reader's benefit and his own.

Ivan Karamazov is a clear embodiment of the atheism and Nihilism that gained popularity during the 1860s in Russia, and Dostoevsky explores Ivan's philosophy more thoroughly than he does with any other character. Through descriptions given by several figures in the opening chapters of *The Brothers Karamazov*, he works out the details of Ivan's theory—as Rakitin puts it, "if there's no immortality of the soul, then there's no virtue, and everything is lawful." (Pt. I, Bk. 2,

Ch. 7) (It is worth noting, however, that one never hears a description of this theory directly from Ivan.) Further, Dostoevsky illustrates the effects of Ivan's beliefs through the actions of Smerdyakov, who admits to their father's murder, but places the blame with Ivan for having taught him that "everything is lawful" in the absence of a God whom Ivan rejects.

Crime and Punishment deals less with Raskolnikov's particular philosophies and more with the *ubermensch* complex that his intellectual pursuits help him to develop. It is this complex that leads him to commit two murders: Leatherbarrow describes Raskolnikov as understanding "crime as the prerogative of a small elite whose value to mankind puts them above punishment or guilt." (139)

It would be easy to think—given the depth of description and painstaking ideological development devoted to Ivan's theories, and the way in which Dostoevsky drags his reader through the thought processes of the murderer Raskolnikov—that he agreed with the ideas espoused by these two characters. It is not difficult to believe that the detailed way in which Dostoevsky catalogues their ideologies mimics the hyperlogical minds of his *ubermensches* precisely because he finds their ways of thinking to be superior and correct. This is particularly true given that Dostoevsky does not offer eloquently developed counterarguments to those of the intellectuals. Even in the legend of the Grand Inquisitor, the mysterious stranger offers no verbal response to the Grand Inquisitor's rationalizing—only a silent kiss. Similarly, though clearly understood as the antithesis of Ivan's atheism, Father Zosima is not a character whose actions or words are organized in opposition to Ivan's elaborate arguments. Zosima does not proselytize or lecture, but instead loves and accepts without question the guilt of the world on his shoulders.

Robert Belknap answers one's anxiety about Dostoevsky's ideological intentions skillfully in his essay, "The Rhetoric of an Ideological Novel," which discusses the action of *The Brothers Karamazov*. The answer he presents is wholly in concert with Dostoevsky's literary structure: Belknap finds that it is precisely Dostoevsky's desire that there *not* be an equally intellectual response to Ivan's Nihilist treatise—that Ivan's intellectualism be answered instead by an opposite and much more ethereal gesture. The kiss given to the Grand Inquisitor—mirrored in the kiss bestowed upon Dmitri by

Father Zosima—is just the sort of "artistic picture" to illustrate Dostoevsky's belief in literary experience over literary statement. (Bloom, 66) Instead of supplying direct arguments, Dostoevsky "cheapens" and undermines Ivan's arguments through the character foils afforded in Rakitin and Kolya. (68) Rather than answering theory with theory, Dostoevsky leads his reader through the experience of an idea in order to find truth. Ivan's Nihilism leads to murder, as does Raskolnikov's intellectual empowerment. It is not difficult to deduce that the reader's *experiences* of these two characters' philosophies are intended to leave him with distaste for the *rationally stated theories* that preceded them.

It is important to note that, though he cast intellectuals at the center of two novels, when attempting to portray the "perfect" man in Prince Myshkin, Dostoevsky did not choose an intellectual.[1] Rather, Myshkin is a man with virtually no education, with a title but without social breeding, who has been away from Russian society for a long length of time but has not been caught up in the "isms" in either Russia or the West. As his choice for a perfect man suggests, Dostoevsky ultimately rejects the intellectual as a false standard for Russian society— a figure too closely related to the powerful Western pressures that were carried into his homeland on the tails of imported philosophies. Given his own words to Maikov and the experiential journeys he creates for his readers, it is apparent that Dostoevsky saw the *true* Russian people as ultimately anti-intellectual, and alternately, highly spiritual.

Dostoevsky's handling of the "woman question"—a phrase oft repeated in *The Idiot* to represent the question of equal rights for women in society, and the related issue of familial breakdown—is only slightly more delicate than his treatment of the Western-influenced intellectual in general. Nina Pelikan Straus sees Dostoevsky's rejection of Western secular theories as inscribing the feminine as sacred: She sees his novels portraying "positive" traditionalist females as redeeming criminal and suffering men, while "new" women "perform ambiguously motivated critiques of traditional masculinity."(2)

It is true that there exists an unmistakable doubling of two feminine types in Dostoevsky's novels. All of his major female characters appear in related pairs: Katerina Ivanovna and Grushenka in *The Brothers Karamazov*; Aglaya and Nastasya Fillipovna in *The Idiot*; Varya and Sonya in *Crime and Punishment*. These pairs include one woman who begins with her propriety but ends up marked as ridiculous, and another who seems fallen from grace but is finally redeemed (though only in death, in the case of Nastasya Fillipovna). Characters such as Aglaya and Katerina Ivanovna, who move from adherence to Russian social morés toward Western intellectualism and liberation, are left looking ridiculous. Having begun as a model of respect, Aglaya rejects the care and security of her "normal" family for the hand of a foreigner and conversion to Catholicism—such an utter rejection of Russian ways leads her only to a laughable marriage and a heretical religion. Katerina Ivanovna is left in an equally undesirable position when her rebellious testimony against her fiancé is revealed as a willful act of revenge for his having rejected her forward behavior.

Alternately, those women who move from a state of scandalous liberty on the fringe of society toward spiritual and social acceptability are capable of redeeming not only themselves, but also the fallen men they love, as in the cases of Grushenka and Sonya.

While Dostoevsky leads his readers to examine the question of women's liberation in such a way that the disruptive outcomes of this trend are highlighted, he does not concoct this experience because of a personal misogyny. His personal commentary on women is unerringly positive. Through a reminiscence of Baron Wrangel, one can hear Dostoevsky's admiration for womankind.

> "Dostoevsky thereupon remarked: 'We should be eternally grateful to a woman whom we have loved, for every day and hour of joy which she as given us. We may not demand from her that she think of us only all her life long; that is ugly egoism, which we should subdue in ourselves.'" (*Letters*, 318)

Indeed, the harsh conclusions that he affords Aglaya and Katerina have more to do with his general belief in the harmful effects of any Western influence—be it toward Nihilism or feminism—and his anxiety that the "woman question" will lead to the downfall of the family, than with a belief that women should be held in a position of submission.

DEATH AND REBIRTH OF SPIRITUALITY

For Fyodor Dostoevsky, to ask the nature of the Russian people was to inquire about their spirituality. In 1880, Dostoevsky wrote, in a letter to Alexander Fyodorovich Blagonravov:

You judge very rightly when you opine that I hold all evil to
be grounded upon disbelief, and maintain that he who
abjures nationalism, abjures faith also. That applies especially
to Russia, for with us national consciousness is based on
Christianity. 'A Christian peasant-people;' 'believing Russia;'
these are our fundamental conceptions. A Russian who
abjures nationalism (and there are many such) is either an
atheist or indifferent to religious questions. And the
converse: an atheist or indifferentist cannot possibly
understand the Russian people and Russian nationalism. The
essential problem of our day is: How are we to persuade our
educated classes of this principle? If one but utters a word in
such a sense, one will either be devoured alive, or denounced
as a traitor.... The first sign of true fellowship with the people
is veneration and love for that which the great mass of the
people loves and venerates—that is to say, for its God and its
faith." (*Letters*, 257–258)

His letter exemplifies the extent to which he saw nationalism and
spiritualism linked in the case of Russia, his desire to see them properly
restored in his day, and his concerns about how to accomplish that
return.

Dostoevsky was raised in the Russian Orthodox church, as were the
vast majority of Russians in his day. As with so many other themes of his
life, his orthodoxy shows through in the details of his novels.
Leatherbarrow notes that the text Father Zosima read as a child is the
same upon which Dostoevsky was raised, *One Hundred and Four Sacred
Stories from the Old and New Testaments Selected for Children*. (150) Not
surprisingly, therefore, Dostoevsky's examination of spirituality is
strongly based in orthodoxy. However, as with the depictions of
intellectualism in his works, his religious contexts are equally informed by
knowledge of other spiritual systems. In preparing to write *The Brothers
Karamazov*, in 1868—then tentatively and tellingly titled *Atheism*—
Dostoevsky revealed to Maikov the extensive investigation into other
religions needed to inform his depiction of Ivan's spiritual struggle.

A long novel entitled, 'Atheism' (but for God's sake, let this
be entirely between ourselves); before I attack it, I shall have

to read a whole library of atheistic works by Catholic and Orthodox-Greek writers." (*Letters*, 157–158)

His research undoubtedly led Dostoevsky to a fuller awareness of other faiths—despite his assumption regarding their ultimate atheism—and perhaps even a partial understanding of their appeal. However, given the exploration and rejection of Western intellectualism throughout his works, one should not be surprised to find Dostoevsky rejecting Western religion—Catholicism and Protestantism—as well. His expanded knowledge informed his works, but only in the sense that it strengthened the experience of questioning and return to orthodox belief that he provided his audience.

Though he always returned to the orthodox context with which he was familiar, one should not deduce that Dostoevsky's personal faith was unwavering. The tentative title of *The Brothers Karamazov* highlights that it is a novel exploring the struggle between religious faith and lack thereof, and the subject matter supports W. J. Leatherbarrow's assertion that, throughout Dostoevsky's life, he found his faith battling the appeal of atheism. (148) He presents the case of atheism particularly well, in fact. As was noted, he explains the Grand Inquisitor's rejection of Christ so convincingly that D.H. Lawrence was persuaded that Dostoevsky was himself an atheist. (Bloom, 53)

It is precisely because of his lingering doubts that Dostoevsky included such potent religious themes in his novels. As we have seen, the questions from life that most haunted Dostoevsky are those which he examined and debated safely in the confines of his literature. Leatherbarrow attributes Dostoevsky's wavering beliefs to his struggle to reconcile his commitment to the church and the image of Christ with his anger over the oppression of the Russian common people. (153)

Dostoevsky's personal religious discontent corresponds to the religious fervor that grew in his literature over time. Religion became increasingly central in the progression of his works, culminating with *The Brothers Karamazov*, which he described as containing "therein my whole heart's burden." (*Letters*, 157)

Malcolm V. Jones, in his essay on "Dostoevskii and Religion," notes that one can see in Dostoevsky's works a process of discovery—or rediscovery—of Christian tradition in the face of its most deadly opponents. (159) Dostoevsky takes on the most bitter opponent to his personal faith, atheism, in such a way that his characters are led just to the brink of losing their faith completely before God and Christian religion are redeemed, and so the reader as well. One is not surprised to find, then, that Ivan Karamazov and Rodion Raskolnikov are redeemed from their Western intellectualism and ultimately return to the Russian Orthodox faith.

Raskolnikov is redeemed through Sonya, a devout youth who endures prostitution for the sake of supporting her family. It is with Sonya that he reads the story of Lazarus, an experience through which he is reborn from his *ubermensch* personality into one of Christian humility. In this rebirth, he leaves behind the intellectual pursuits that first inspired him to sin.

Dostoevsky leaves Ivan Karamazov with a less obvious, but no less certain, path to redemption. At the close of *The Brothers Karamazov*, Ivan lies sick with brain fever, and the words of the narrator make it unclear whether he will survive. Should he survive, explains the narrator, Ivan will redeem himself by saving his innocent brother, Dmitri, from unwarranted servitude, abandoning his intellectual pursuits in favor of a Christian life; but this redemption is not illustrated in such clear terms. Nonetheless, a potential clue to Dostoevsky's intentions for Ivan lies in the name given to the character: Dostoevsky provided his greatest sinner with a name that connotes rebirth. While the surname Karamazov means "black smear," the name Ivan is the Russian equivalent to the English John, one of Christ's disciples, and "Ivan" is translated in Russian as "divine grace" or "god's gift." (Passage, 95) Dostoevsky's choice of the name Ivan/John gains greater importance when considered in the context of his dedication to the novel, which features a passage from John 12:24.

> "Verily, verily, I say unto you, Except a corn of wheat fall into the ground and die, it abideth alone, but if it die, it bringeth forth much fruit."

The biblical passage highlights the necessity of spiritual demise—a process paralleled in Ivan's journey through atheism to the brink of death—in order for a soul to blossom in its full glory. Thus, though he begins the novel marked with a black smear of disbelief, Ivan is left on the path to redemption, with the reader hoping that he will rise to follow it, knowing that he is capable, but not able to witness this wholly personal rebirth.

Dostoevsky understood the importance of seeing and experiencing an issue from the viewpoint of another, and did so himself to understand nonorthodox spirituality. The value he placed on experiencing multiple viewpoints is related to a belief—illustrated in Father Zosima and, ultimately, Dmitri Karamazov—that all are responsible for the guilt of one. The structure of his literature not only leads his readers to question spirituality, but lets them move through the experiences and ideas of multiple characters to better understand the sins of others. In due course, if the consciousness Dostoevsky creates in his works is understood as he intended, his readers come to an understanding that they must take those sins upon themselves, as Father Zosima took on the sins of the world.

CONCLUSION

Dostoevsky's desire to represent a fundamental spiritual experience—taking his heroes, and with them, his readers, to the depths of doubt before leading them back toward faith—clearly informed his literary structure, one that facilitates exploration of foreign experiences without leading the reader to foregone conclusions.

As the nature of his spirituality influenced his literary structure, it also determined his nationalistic rejection of Western ideologies—not as unsound in their foreign nature, but impossibly counter to the Russian spirituality he held dear.

Dostoevsky knew, from the moment of his pardon, "that matters of faith were not peripheral to living and dying, but vitally relevant to every minute of his experience." (Leatherbarrow, 154) However, his understanding that faith is and must be intimately connected to all other aspects of one's life did not keep him from questioning God and Christianity. Instead, it led to lifelong exploration of alternative modes of thinking, all of which both challenged and reinforced his spirituality. This is what one ultimately finds in Dostoevsky's works: an open-ended spiritual exploration, one fraught with uncertainty, that challenges and reinforces a belief in God and the goodness of man, but that does not ultimately provide closure in any direction. For, there is no point in living once the questions are gone.

NOTE

1. In a letter to his niece, Sofia Alexandrovna Dostoevsky, in 1868, Fyodor Dostoevsky described "the basic idea" of his most recent work, *The Idiot*, as "the representation of a truly perfect and noble man." (*Letters*, 142)

WORKS CITED

Bakhtin, Mikhail. *Problems of Dostoevsky's Poetics*. Ann Arbor: Ardis, 1973.

Bloom, Harold, ed. *Modern Critical Interpretations: The Brothers Karamazov*. New York: Chelsea House Publishers, 1988.

Dostoevsky, Fyodor. *Letters of Fyodor Michailovitch Dostoevsky to His Family and Friends*. London: Chatto & Windus, 1914.

Engelstein, Laura and Stephanie Sandler, eds. *Self and Story in Russian History*. Ithaca: Cornell University Press, 2000.

Grossman, Leonid. *Dostoevsky: A Biography*. London: Allen Lane, 1974.

Leatherbarrow, W.J., ed. *The Cambridge Companion to Dostoevksii*. Cambridge: Cambridge University Press, 2002.

Passage, Charles E. *Character Names in Dostoevsky's Fiction*. Ann Abor: Ardis, 1982.

Straus, Nina Pelikan. *Dostoevsky and the Woman Question: Rereadings at the End of a Century*. New York: St. Martin's Press, 1994.

Terras, Victor. *Reading Dostoevksy*. Madison: University of Wisconsin Press, 1998.

WILLIAM MILLS TODD III

Storied Selves: Constructing Characters *in* The Brothers Karamazov

For a volume on "self and story" in Russian history, a study of Dostoevsky's last novel, *The Brothers Karamazov* (Brat'ia Karamazovy, 1881), which foregrounds its characters' uses and misuses of narrative as they attempt to understand the extreme possibilities of human behavior, offers many opportunities to reflect on both "self" and "story." In this essay I will outline a reading of the novel that focuses upon the central themes of this volume, illuminating them with modern theories of narrative which share Dostoevsky's own fascination with self and story. To the extent that *The Brothers Karamazov* constitutes not only a reflection on narrative in general but criticism of the kinds of story told by its culture, I will suggest how it can help make us aware of the ways late nineteenth-century Russians told stories. Here I will use modern theories of narrative to discuss the novel's own problematization of narrative, which is itself part of a long tradition in literature and in critical reflection.

Since Greek antiquity selves and stories have been inextricably intertwined in accounts of both "self" (or its rough equivalents) and "story." Our earliest theory of narrative, Aristotle's *Poetics*, may not entertain the notion of "self" in a recognizably modern sense, but it does have to deal with human agency in discussing actions, it does consider the social position of these agents, and it does endow them with

From *Self and Story in Russian History* edited by Laura Engelstein and Stephanie Sandler. © 2000 by Cornell University Press. Reprinted with permission of Cornell University Press.

character traits.[1] Subsequent theories, such as Propp's, at the very least
entertain the first of these hypostases of character, the notion of agency.
But most, whether normative or descriptive, will attempt to do more:
dictate the types of characters most appropriate to a particular kind of
narrative; posit what makes a character interesting or capable of
generating narrative curiosity; study how characters can be constructed
in narratives. Our most ornate and brilliant theory of narrative, Roland
Barthes' *S/Z*, giving play to myriad critical discourses, jargons, and terms
only to be found in a Greek dictionary, nevertheless makes problems of
character and human agency central to the working of his five narrative
codes.[2] Indeed, reversing the focus on action that has been the rule since
Aristotle, Barthes argues that it is this movement of traits toward a
proper name, not action, that is the property of narrative.[3] In plainer
English, narrative becomes a process of endowing proper names with
character. In any event, Barthes preserves and expands Aristotle's
understandings of literary personages as agents, characters, and
functions of context.

When we move from narrative in general to its principal modern
literary manifestation, the novel, we see that theories of the novel are to
an even greater degree fixated upon character, emphasizing to a greater
degree, as is historically appropriate, issues of individuation and
consciousness. Georg Lukács's famous inquiry defines novelistic plotting
in terms of the movements and understandings of character: the
"outward form" of the novel is the biography of a problematic
individual, whose individuality is an end unto itself in a contingent
world, while what Lukács calls the "inner form" of the novel is the
problematic individual's journey toward self-recognition. "Outward"
and "inner" in each case focus upon an individual.[4] Lukács's Russian
contemporary, Mikhail Bakhtin, was drawn to and challenged such a
conception of the novel, developing a number of different insights about
narrative which explode the traditions of plot oriented Aristotelian
poetics. Speech, not action, becomes the center of Bakhtin's focus in his
most developed essay, "Discourse in the Novel," and the "speaking
person" becomes the novel's hero. But for all of Bakhtin's indifference to
plotting in a traditional sense of the ordering of events, the testing or
challenging of the hero in his theory of the novel do enter into a sort of
master plot, the process of the speaking person's "coming to know his or
her own language as it is perceived in someone else's language, coming

to know one's own belief system in someone else's system."[5] "Story," in short, has become inconceivable without not just actors or products of cultural contexts but also without "selves," individuated and coherent in varying degrees, depending on the theory in question.

But "self" is scarcely less conceivable without "story" in most modern treatments. Where it once may have been adequate to describe a character by measuring a person against an established norm or by attaching traits to a proper name—no small process of individuation, given that Webster's gives nearly 18,000 trait names[6]—a modern sense of self generally involves development over time. And the depiction of development over time inevitably calls forth narrative, our principal cognitive means, as Louis Mink has put it, for making comprehensive the many successive interrelationships that are composed by a career.[7] Cathy Popkin's paper for this volume shows how medical science of the late nineteenth century used narrative to constitute character according to disciplinary rules. We do not need to rehearse here the many different ways in which our various schools of psychoanalysis and developmental psychology construct, or deconstruct, individuated or integral selves, normative life histories, or case studies. The point is that all do this in story form.

Distinctions suggested by the novel itself aid our inquiry. These distinctions, in narratological terms, address three aspects of the poetics and pragmatics of narrative: the *plot*, the ordering of events and personages; the *narration*, the teller's presentation of events and personages; and the *reception*, the reader's or listener's processing of the story. The first aspect, plot, involves the openness of the story, the play that it allows for the subject's agency, potential, and own definition of self. It also involves the scope of the story: Is it a general account or a particular story? The whole story of the self, or just a part? The second aspect, narration, involves, primarily, distance and engagement: Is the story told with scientific objectivity, from a distance, or with varying kinds of personal involvement (egocentric/selfless) with the object of discourse? A related set of distinctions, ones involving the ideological involvement of the narrator, sets secular discourse against the insights of faith (scientific objectivity/loving empathy). The third aspect of the novel's stories of the self, reception, involves the participation of the listener, for many of these stories are told orally to personages, in their physical presence, making them the objects of dialogue, often heated or abusive.

The Brothers Karamazov, serialized over a two-year period in one of Russia's leading "thick journals" (1879–80), represents a field where Russia's various stories for constituting selves could, and did, confront each other. Or, more precisely, a field within a field, for the thick journals themselves, by bringing together fiction and literary reviews with articles on a variety of historical, scientific, and social-scientific topics, themselves forced confrontations between the discourses of Russia's incipient professions and academic disciplines. We may borrow the prosecutor's simile, "like the sun in a small drop of water," in turn borrowed from Derzhavin, to suggest this process of miniaturization, by which contemporary ways of characterizing the self come together first in the period's popular journals, then in Dostoevsky's last novel.[8] During the two years of serialization alone, *The Russian Herald* (Russkii vestnik) sandwiched the installments of *The Brothers Karamazov* among articles, many of them also serialized, on natural and physical science, military history, imperial history (the Polish and Eastern questions), religion, travel, the law (courts and prison reform), pedagogy, economics, music, art, and literature.[9] Contemporary readers of the novel would have these subjects before their eyes from this journal alone, to say nothing about what they would have encountered in rival thick journals, such as *The Herald of Europe* (Vestnik Evropy), *National Annals* (Otechestvennye zapiski), *Deed (Delo)*, and *Russian Wealth* (Russkoe bogatstvo). The increasingly popular daily newspapers of the 1870s had come to carry the greater part of court and crime reporting, although Dostoevsky's one-man journal, *Diary of a Writer* (Dnevnik pisatelia), treated a number of trials at length as well as many of the social, cultural, and foreign-policy controversies of the time.[10] But Dostoevsky established a further journalistic context for his readers by setting his novel in the postreform late 1860s, when the journals—which then included *The Contemporary* (Sovremennik) and the Dostoevsky brothers' *Time* (Vremia) and *Epoch* (Epokha)—devoted more space to discussion of the judicial reforms as well as to deterministic theories of human development, such as we encounter in the novel in the writings and dialogue of the journalist Rakitin in *The Brothers Karamazov*.

The prosecutor accompanies his simile, however, with a specular metaphor: "in the picture of this fine little family it is as if certain general fundamental elements of our contemporary intellectual society may be glimpsed—oh, not all the elements, and in microscopic view, 'like the sun in a small drop of water,' yet something has been reflected in it."[11] If one must have an optical metaphor, I would prefer "refracted," because it seems that when the novel deals with contemporary ways of storying the self, it does so by bending and ordering them from a particular angle, much as a prism would bend and order the intensities of a stream of light.

Through this prism of novelistic discourse the self becomes indeed storied, not only in the sense of the object and subject of stories, but also by being layered, as in the stories of a house. The personages of the novel become subject to many kinds of story, some literary, some scientific, some social-scientific. But we are never allowed to forget the angles of refraction, that stories are told by someone, to someone, and, instrumentally, for some purpose. This manifest refracting of stories of the self is evident from the opening pages of the novel, the passage "From the Author," which is generally ignored in the critical discourse. Here a sarcastic, maddeningly indefinite author figure presents Alesha, the youngest of the Karamazov brothers, from several different angles: as hero of the novel, as a character possibly not grand enough to play this role, as an indefinite figure, and as an eccentric, a special case, yet one which might represent "the heart of the whole" more than the other people of the era.[12] The author is fussy, hostile, on the edge of that aggressive buffoonery which character-narrators (Fedor, Maksimov, Ivan's devil, the defense attorney) will later adopt, on the edge of that clumsy, excited, at times ungrammatical, discourse that Valentina Vetlovskaia has accurately attributed to the novel's primary narrator.[13] This author figure's only solution to the problems he poses, including those of character, is his refusal to solve them. He makes a mockery of the notion that literature imitates reality by treating both text and reality in terms of senselessness and confusion (*bestoloch'*). Every aspect of the text, he promises, will be either ambiguous or muddled: its genre, both "biography" and "novel"; the hero, an unheroic eccentric; and its structure—it begins with a preface the author calls superfluous yet nevertheless includes, and its significance will become clear only from the sequel, which the author does not, of course, include. The reader, assaulted by these equivocations, ambiguities, and muddles, finds him or herself projected, sarcastically, as one who will disagree with the "author," will have to guess at what the author is trying to say, and may even read through to the end, unlike the sixty or so unnamed "Russian critics" who took it upon themselves to review the novel before serialization was completed.[14] As a provocation to the reader, the narrator's own disjointed narrative becomes purposeful. The structure of the book will provide many patterns of repetition to guide the reader, as Robert Belknap has noted, and some of the book's characters, primarily Alesha and Zosima, will successfully "read" the other characters' stories with a measure of insight.[15] But these characters, whose insight is not infallible, will be the closest a reader comes to finding positive models of narrative reception in the text. The other characters, as narrators and listeners to narrative, provide only negative guidance: how *not* to process narrative and how *not* to understand character.

The author figure yields to the primary narrator as the novel opens, but "senselessness and confusion" echo from its opening pages through to the great trial scene in the novel's last book. Not the least of these enigmas concerns character, and the older two brothers, Dmitri and Ivan, represent its greatest mysteries and greatest breadth in the novel, with the principal female characters, Grushenka and Katerina Ivanovna, coming close behind. Dmitri poses the question most extravagantly, characterizing Ivan as a "tomb" and humanity a "riddle" and launching into his own refraction, in extravagantly aesthetic terms, of the spectrum of human capabilities:

> God sets us nothing but riddles. There the shores meet and all contradictions coexist…. It's terrible how many mysteries there are! Too many riddles weigh men down on earth. We must solve them as we can, and try to come out of the water with a dry skin. Beauty! I can't bear it that a man of lofty mind and heart begins with the ideal of the Madonna and ends with the ideal of Sodom. What's still more terrifying is that a man with the ideal of Sodom in his soul does not renounce the ideal of the Madonna, and his heart may be on fire with that ideal, genuinely on fire, just as in his days of youth and innocence. No, man is broad, too broad, indeed. I'd narrow him.[16]

The movement of the novel involves the reader in a quest to resolve these enigmas, as it does the characters. Multiple narrations construct incidents in different ways, indexing the characters with different traits. Dmitri himself will provide the richest examples, as he finds himself, even in the opening parts of the novel, the object of five different narrations of the thrashing of Captain Snegirev: by Fedor, who omits the specific nature of the captain's business; twice by Dmitri, who ignores the captain's lamentable family situation; once by Katerina Ivanovna, who adds the presence of the captain's son, and, finally, in excruciating detail by the captain himself, who adds Dmitri's viciously humiliating offer to fight a duel. Depending on the version, Dmitri comes off as noble officer, brute, or sadist—i.e., as the military equivalent of one who bears the ideal of Madonna or the ideal of Sodom. At the end of the novel, when he is tried for parricide, Dmitri will again be the object of multiple narrations, emerging with a similar range of "selves" from the narratives, of lawyers, doctors, and witnesses.

Many of these stories collapse in utter futility; some—for the characters and perhaps for the reader—have the ring of truth. In a novel legendary for its ambiguities and confusion, how are these stories of the self ordered? Which emerge as plausible? By what criteria? Does the novel, adopting the grand ambitions of nineteenth-century science, posit laws by which the self may be known? Probabilities? Possibilities? Or does it, rejecting even the most modest of these conclusions, undermine all the stories by which the self might be known? Who pretends to story the self, by what authority, and how? Some of the answers involve recognizable scientific discourses, at times in the mouths of licensed representatives of Russia's incipient professions (such as lawyers or doctors), at times in the reports of educated laymen (such as the narrator or the journalist-seminarian Rakitin). It is not possible to account for every story told in *The Brothers Karamazov*, but we may essay some observations on these stories' attempts to deal with the characters of the novel.

Among the discourses the novel examines are those in which the observer tries to penetrate the secrets of the self and still, to borrow Dmitri's image, "come out of the water with a dry skin": medicine and "psychology." These attempts range from typification (as in the narrator's learned discussion of the abused women who become "shriekers") to specific diagnoses (the famous Moscow doctor's prescriptions for Iliusha, the court psychiatrists). Such stories told in the absence of the subject may have the ring of plausibility, as when the narrator explains the calming effect of the Eucharist on an hysterical peasant woman:

> The strange and instantaneous healing of the possessed and struggling woman as soon as she was led up to the holy sacrament, which had been explained to me as pretense and even trickery arranged by the "clericals," arose probably in the most natural manner.... With a nervous and psychically ill woman, a sort of convulsion of the whole organism inevitably took place at the moment of bowing before the sacrament, aroused by expectation of the inevitable miracle of healing and the fullest belief that it would come to pass; and it did come to pass, though only for a moment.[17]

The narrator's sympathy for the hard lot of rural women, expressed in the philanthropic terms of a socially and culturally superior observer, his eschewal of an easy cynical explanation (a show staged by the clergy), and his rational, psychological account of irrational behavior make this explanation persuasive. At this relatively early point in the novel (Book Two, Chapter Three) we have nothing to contradict either its explanatory power or the narrator's credibility. Indeed, the early chapters feature a number of such commonsensical explanations, which the novel has not yet taught its readers to distrust. The narrator's presentation of Fedor Karamazov's first wife abounds in such explanations: "Adelaida Ivanovna's behavior was without doubt the echo of foreign influences, also the irritation from thought imprisoned. She perhaps wished to display female independence, to go against social conventions, against the despotism of her relatives and family."[18] The reader's subsequent acquaintance with the characters of the novel will reveal the superficiality and inadequacy of such seemingly plausible cultural, social, and psychological explanations.

Indeed, as the novel continues, commonsense psychological explanations become nuanced and undermined. Hysteria, for instance, becomes the property of all classes—and genders—of the novel's characters, and it is far from easily calmed by any treatment. Ultimately, the more rational—and the more scientific or professionalized—the story of sickness, the less adequate it becomes. The old German doctor, Herzenstube, is absolutely helpless as a physician, but his kindness touches Dmitri and is remembered by him. The district doctor, Varvinskii, is fooled by Smerdiakov, Markel's doctor mistakes religious enlightenment for brain fever, the confession of Zosima's mysterious visitor is taken for madness. The famous Moscow doctor's prescriptions for the impoverished Snegirev family create for them an absurd story that is cruelly impossible to live out: travel to Syracuse for Iliusha, to the Caucasus for Nina, to the Caucasus and to Paris for the mother. Medical science reaches the height of absurdity at the trial, where three doctors (Herzenstube, the Moscow specialist, and Varvinskii) debate the direction in which Dmitri, if sane, should have looked upon entering the court, to the left, to the right, or straight ahead.[19]

Ultimately the medical narratives, like the psychological ones, are subservient to the legal process, which brings not only the characters but also their stories together in the last, and longest, book of the novel. Here the reader sees that the plots and characters created by the novel's police investigators and attorneys likewise fail to come to grips with the breadth of the novel's personages. The story that the district attorney and his colleagues put together during the preliminary investigation (Book Nine) is based on their assumptions and on Grigorii's faulty evidence as well as on what they can squeeze out of the exhausted, ecstatic Dmitri. It is remarkable for its deductive logic: they have decided that Dmitri is guilty, therefore they will assemble what they need to confirm that the murder is a rational, premeditated act. Dmitri counters their story of him with "his own story," as he calls it, that of an honorable officer who has had some difficulties, but who has not become a thief and who has been saved from murdering his father by his guardian angel. Dmitri's story lacks coherence, to say nothing of the weight of institutional authority, and it cannot counteract the police account of him as a rational killer. A third story of Dmitri's character is constructed during this investigation, however, this time by the narrator with help from the reader's ability to remember previous detail; this emerging story compares the former Dmitri to the one who develops during his ordeals. The new Dmitri still bears the traits of recklessness and impulsiveness but, as is seen in his dream of the baby, has compassion and concern for the suffering of others. His vision occurs toward the end of the interrogation, a process which has a profound moral impact upon him, stripping him of his superiority and his superficial sense of honor, the sense of honor that had, we may recall, led him to invite the helpless Snegirev to challenge him to a duel. As Dmitri is quite literally stripped, he loses his old attachments to life and turns, ever so slowly, toward new ones. It is, after all, hard to feel proud and superior in dirty socks and underwear.

The narratives constructed by the attorneys in the trial only compound the inadequacy of the preliminary investigation by adding the expert testimony of medical science and amateurish social science. Under Russia's recently instituted adversarial system, a trial had become a contest between storytellers, as Dostoevsky had pointed out in his journalistic pieces and demonstrates here, in Book Twelve of *The Brothers Karamazov*. To gain a conviction, the prosecution had to construct an airtight narrative in which some criminal event took place and its willing agent was the defendant. The defense was given a different storytelling task. To create the necessary grain of doubt, it had to break the prosecution's narrative down by showing that there was no criminal event or chain of events, or by showing that even if there was, the defendant was not the agent of these events.

In this trial both attorneys cut corners in their research and argumentation. The form of the story overwhelms its content; fiction-making talent comes to the fore. The narrator, lawyers, and witnesses use, in fact, a variety of literary terms to describe the trial and its arguments: "tragic," "comedy," "scenario," "spectacle," "fiction," "novel," "legend," "drama."[20] The prosecutor begins with the conclusion to the plot (that Dmitri with premeditation killed his father) and builds the story accordingly: this involves dismissing the intelligence, stability, and character of Dmitri's three witnesses (Alesha, Ivan, Grushenka). It involves constructing Dmitri's character to suit the plot and finalizing that character. For the prosecutor to tell us that there is a "real" Dmitri Karamazov ignores Dmitri's development and range of possibilities. Using this fictitious "real Dmitri," the prosecutor in turn shapes the events of the murder plot. This implicates Dmitri in a series of hypothetical actions which, as the reader by now knows, did not take place: Dmitri gradually spending the reserve of money, for instance. As if Dmitri could do such things in small installments! Or Dmitri consciously hiding the remaining 1500 rubles in Mokroe. As if Dmitri could have been concerned with anything but Grushenka at that moment. Ivan, whom the reader has seen undergoing the most profound transformation in the novel, is similarly grist for the prosecutor's mill.

We see the prosecutor questioning why Ivan did not immediately come forth to report Smerdiakov's confession. The demands of legal narrative require that the prosecutor make Ivan a calculating, dishonorable slanderer of the dead, not a man wracked with guilt—and the prosecutor does precisely this. Finally, and pivotally, the prosecutor must, ventriloquized by Smerdiakov himself, construct a suitable biography and character for the only plausible alternative murderer, Smerdiakov. And in the prosecutor's "treatise on Smerdiakov" we see him doing just this. The result is a timid, sickly, "naturally honest" Smerdiakov who couldn't possibly have committed the crime that we know by this time he did commit. The prosecutor's loaded words in this treatise— "psychology," "fact," "natural"—conceal the extent to which psychology, fact, and nature are the prosecutor's narrative constructs, constructs that he has assembled in accordance with his needs and institutional requirements, constructs that he has borrowed wholesale from the murderer.

The defense attorney, Fetiukovich, adopts a different narrative strategy and tells a different story, using many of the same acts and actors. But, predictably, he provides different contexts and puts the acts and actors into different chins of events, drawing on different traits to characterize his personages. His institutional role requires him to see sudden acts and incoherence where the prosecution sees deliberate thought and action. Thus the "talented" Fetiukovich gives priority to acts and actors as potential plot material, not as products of his need for a particular outcome. He attacks the "whole logic of the prosecution." He dismantles the "combination of facts." And he reverses the psychology of all the characters, drawing on his famous maxim that "psychology is a two-edged weapon." To this end he employs his "talent" for humor, ridicule, and deconstructive logic. He takes each building block of the prosecutor's narrative—each character, each event—and gives it a different spin, a different place in a different story. Countering the dead certainty of the prosecutor's account and its determinism, which is based on notions of both the Karamazovs' heredity and their environment, the wily defense attorney constructs character and action in ways closer to the understandings of the loving Christian figures, Zosima and Alesha, namely, character as open construct and actions as sudden, spontaneous. Thus Fetiukovich makes Smerdiakov a much more clever, complex character than does the prosecutor, and this is, in fact, closer to the truth. Does this make Fetiukovich a spokesman for Dostoevsky? Or does it make him similar to Dostoevsky's greatest liar, General Ivolgin in *The Idiot*, who happened to tell the truth once, by accident? It is probably the latter. Fetiukovich's job is to sow doubt, not to tell the truth. His narrative, like the prosecutor's, is still a fiction, although a more modern, sophisticated one.

As these narratives, ostensibly created in the service of truth and justice, become increasingly a matter of personal competition between the attorneys, as, indeed, the medical experts' testimony had been a matter of personal pride and competition, we must turn to the second of the three aspects of narrative that the novel foregrounds, the teller's role in the story. The defense attorney's own term for the story with which he concludes his speech is "hypothesis"—i.e., an unproven fiction which might capture reality. This is a term that Kolia Krasotkin uses, as does Ivan Karamazov. It implies an intellectual detachment from life, from empathy. And here it becomes a masterpiece of equivocation on Fetiukovich's part. It is not enough for him to discredit the witnesses and to deconstruct the prosecution's story. He must become a romance writer himself. And so he reaches out to argue that there was no robbery and no murder. He must put his talent for rhetoric and casuistry to the ultimate test, to argue before a jury of patriarchal Russians that even if Dmitri murdered his father, it really did not count as parricide, because Fedor had not been a real father to him. One could only call it murder out of "prejudice." Fetiukovich concludes his speech with notions of salvation, penitence, regeneration, and resurrection, but the damage is done. He has been swept away by his talent, and both prosecutor and jury recoil from his flamboyant hypothesis by convicting Dmitri.

It is possible to argue that the defense attorney here is trying to mitigate Dmitri's guilt. Under the postreform judicial procedures, a simple majority of jurors could have called for clemency. But I would argue that Fetiukovich's argument is more a case of ego run amok, of the inspired lying one so often encounters in Dostoevsky's characters. The motives and interests behind his storytelling are clearly competitive and aesthetic. His wildly applauded performance is answered by Dmitri's simple but dignified final statement, in which he refuses to recognize himself in either lawyer's account.

This ineluctably self-interested aspect of the attorneys' stories is but a special case of most of the novel's stories; the teller's egocentricity becomes, paradoxically, most evident in those discourses that pretend to the greatest distance and objectivity. Not only are stories told in the professionalized discourses (medicine, psychology, law), then, limited by the rules of the profession, they are also limited by the vanity, competitiveness, and hostility of the speaker. This holds true for the journalists' discourse as well, that of both Ivan and Rakitin. The "little pictures" of Ivan's attack on God's world, culled from the newspapers, nevertheless are marshaled in an argument the basic aim of which is an attack on Alesha's faith and an attempt, momentarily successful, to seduce him to share in Ivan's unforgiving hostility. Rakitin's explanations in terms of heredity and environment, which so influence the prosecutor, emerge from the novel's refraction as the products of his greed, ambition, and resentment of Ivan. In each case any attempt to tell a truthful story is overshadowed by deeply personal attempts to exercise power or to gain vengeance. This, in turn, further compromises the professional discourses, which already appear inadequate for their rule-bound, limited view of the self.

Much of the dynamism of a Dostoevsky novel, and this one in particular, derives from the third aspect of stories of the self, their reception. Even the most silent listener to a story of the self, Christ before the Grand Inquisitor, makes a gesture of response, the kiss that may signify the forgiveness which undercuts the Grand Inquisitor's argument. The novel's nondivine characters typically respond more violently and vociferously to the storied selves which other characters create for them. From the beginning of the novel to the end, examples abound of these rebellious rejections of another's story—present, past, or future—about oneself. Fedor increases his buffoonery and lying after Zosima proposes to him that he try to stop. Grushenka turns savagely against Katerina Ivanovna because she refused to be the person Katerina Ivanovna wanted her to be; Grushenka refused to play the necessary part in Katerina Ivanovna's dream, as Dmitri astutely and gleefully notes: "She truly fell in love with Grushenka, that is, not with Grushenka, but with her own dream, her own delusion—because it was her own dream, her own delusion."[21] Captain Snegirev suddenly rejects and tramples a much-needed two-hundred-ruble gift from Katerina Ivanovna at the very moment when Alesha, his interlocutor, unthinkingly inserts himself into a story of the captain's future life, as Alesha subsequently comes to realize.[22] The captain tramples the money in trying to escape precisely that characterization of him which Alesha offers to Lise ("he is a cowardly man and weak in character"). Down to the last pages of the novel, when we see Dmitri railing against Claude Bernard, the famous French physician who was a darling of the journalists of the 1860s for his physiological explanations of human behavior, we see the novel's personages reject any sort of contextualization, any attribution of traits, or any assigned roles in another's narrative. They are quick to insist that these are not the whole story or the true story, and if the story seems too whole or true, they will do something to contradict it or otherwise show its inadequacy. The novel, then, develops a *negative* poetics for stories of the self, which its characters emphatically reject: excessive narratorial distance, egocentric narratorial involvement, rigid master plots, formal rules. Such plot schemes and ways of telling finalize character, they preclude agency and unexpected change on the part of the characters in the narratives, and they fail to allow for the possibility of unexpected change-producing events, such as Dmitri's vision of the baby.

Zosima's teachings, as they are constructed by Alesha in Book Six of the novel, offer an implicit *positive* poetics for the creation of stories that might be acceptable and effective: his teachings about the need for erasing the difference between servants and masters, his teaching about the interconnectedness of all, about the mutual responsibility of all for all, about mysterious seeds from other worlds all imply stories that would lack a hierarchy or distance among teller, subject, and listener; they suggest tellers as open to change and new understanding as the characters they are constructing; they remind us of Yuri Lotman's point that "events" are happenings that did not have to happen.[23]

Alesha's final speech once again adumbrates this positive poetics— indeed, ethics—of narration. It appeals to narrative, making Iliusha's life into an exemplary narrative which might be joined to the future narratives of his own and the boys' lives, and it appeals for narrative, the expression of the memory that will be a moral force not only for these young people; but for Alesha himself. Here Alesha does not, as narrator, separate himself from the events and characters of this concluding story, for to do so would manifest the negative poetics and pragmatics of narration which the novel has so rigorously exposed.

At the same time, however, the world of the novel shows its readers that even this ideal narrative communication, with its open endings and unfinalized characters, can be strenuously resisted by its characters, whose suspicions and fears can lead them to see coercion and fixity. Zosima's life is filled with characters who have accepted stories— Markel, Zosima himself, Zosima's mysterious visitor—but it is not easy even for these parable-like figures to accept the "spiritual, psychological" process of transformation, supported by active love.[24] Of the Karamazov brothers, only Alesha seems to have accepted it by the novel's end. Ivan is suffering from brain fever; Dmitri realizes that his acceptance of grace is at best fragile.

Toward the very beginning of Dostoevsky's writing career, in 1847, his early supporter and critic, Belinsky, wrote: "With us the personality is just beginning to break out of its shell."[25] Dostoevsky's mature writings would show both how difficult it was to break out of that shell, and how inadequately the regnant discourses of his day described the process for personalities who would accept neither the traits, nor the contexts, nor the roles that these discourses assigned them. Stories and selves fit very poorly together in Dostoevsky's novels, which transform learned treatises into fiction, narrators into liars, and listeners into resentful rebels, especially when the stories concern themselves. The more authoritative, rule-governed, and professionalized the narrative, the more likely it is to fail its subject and object, generating in turn new stories. Whether addressing the memorably resilient selves of its characters or turning outward to reflect on history, thought, and culture, *The Brothers Karamazov* never lets its readers forget that stories are never detached, nor disinterested, nor predictably instrumental. Yet the simple fact that Dostoevsky included his critique of narrative within a narrative, a lengthy novel, testifies to the inescapability of storytelling in coming to grips with the elusive self, It also testifies to his hope that teller and reader might, at last, get the story right.

Attention to the terms and debates of narrative theory illuminates the complexities of Dostoevsky's storied selves. Multiple refractions await even the dimmest ray of narrative light. Turning outward from literature and literary theory to Russian history, politics, and culture, Dostoevsky's novel reminds its readers that the stories one tells are part of a process in which the role stories play is neither detached, nor disinterested, nor predictably instrumental.

NOTES

1. For a discussion of Aristotle's treatment of character, see Seymour Chatman, *Story and Discourse: Narrative Structure in Fiction anti Film* (Ithaca: Cornell University Press, 1978), 108–10.

2. The hermeneutic code, by which enigmas are posed and resolved, clearly deals with problems of human identity; the proairetic code, which governs actions, presupposes (as in Aristotle and Propp) human actors; the symbolic code organizes character as a function of rhetorical figures and tropes, such as antithesis; the cultural code views character as the product of regnant understandings, such as popular psychology; and the semic code attaches traits to a proper name. See Roland Barthes, *S/Z: An Essay*, trans. Richard Miller (New York: Hill and Wang, 1974).

3. Barthes, *S/Z*, 191.

4. Georg Lukács, *The Theory of the Novel* (Cambridge, Mass.: MIT Press, 1971), 77–80.

5. M.M. Bakhtin, *The Dialogic Imagination: Four Essays*, trans. Caryl Emerson and Michael Holquist (Austin: University of Texas Press, 1981), 365. Cf. Bakhtin's notion of "ideological becoming": the process of selectively assimilating the words of others, of liberating oneself from the authority of another's discourse, 341–48.

6. Chatman, *Story and Discourse*, 125 n38.

7. Louis Mink, "Narrative Form as a Cognitive Instrument," in R. Canary and H. Kozicki, ed., *The Writing of History: Literary Form and Historical Understanding* (Madison: University of Wisconsin Press, 1977), 134.

8. F.M. Dostoevskii, *Polnoe sobranie sochinenii v tridtsati tomakh* (Leningrad: Nauka, 1972–90), 15: 125.

9. For a more detailed account of this phenomenon, see William Mills Todd III, "*The Brothers Karamazov* and the Poetics of Serial Publication," *Dostoevsky Studies* 7 (1986): 87–97.

10. For information on Dostoevsky and the court reporting of the time, see David Keily, "*The Brothers Karamazov* and the Fate of Russian Truth: Shifts in the Construction and Interpretation of Narrative After the Judicial Reform of 1864," Ph.D. diss., Harvard University, 1996; also T. C. Karlova, *Dostoevskii i russkii sud* (Kazan: Izdatel'stvo Kazanskogo Universiteta, 1975).

11. Dostoevskii, *Polnoe sobranie sochinenii*, 15: 125.

12. Ibid., 14: 5.

13. V.E. Vetlovskaia, *Poetika romana "Brat'ia Karamazovy"* (Leningrad: Nauka, 1977), 34–39.

14. For a survey of these reviews, see William Mills Todd III, "Contexts of Criticism: Reviewing *The Brothers Karamazov* in 1879," *Stanford Slavic Studies* 4, no. 1 (1991): 293–310.

15. Robert L. Belknap, *The Structure of* The Brothers Karamazov (Evanston: Northwestern University Press, 1989). On the function of memory in the novel's poetics, see Diane Oenning Thompson, The Brothers Karamazov *and the Poetics of Memory* (Cambridge: Cambridge University Press, 1991).

16. Dostoevskii, *Polnoe sobranie sochinenii*, 14: 104.

17. Ibid., 14: 44.

18. Ibid., 14: 8.

19. Ibid., 15: 103–7.

20. The Russian word *roman* can be translated either as "novel" or as "romance." For an exploration of the storytelling manner of the two attorneys, see W. Wolfgang Holdheim, *Der Justizirztum als literarische Problematik vergleichende Analyse eines erzahlerischen Themas* (Berlin: De Gruyter, 1969). A large and growing body of contributions to the "law and literature" movement in legal studies has begun to address problems of legal narrative, although rarely drawing on the full complexity of narrative theory. For an exception, with useful bibliography, see Keily, "*The Brothers Karamazov* and the Fate of Russian Truth."

21. Dostoevskii, *Polnoe sobranie sochinenii*, 14: 143.

22. Ibid., 14: 196.

23. Iu. M. Lotman, *Struktura khudozhestvennogo teksta* (Providence: Brown University Press, 1971), 285.

24. Dostoevskii, *Polnoe sobranie sochinenii*, 14: 175.

25. V.G. Belinskii, *Polnoe sobranie sochinenii v deviati tomakh* (Moscow: Khudozhestvennaia literatura, 1976–82), 9: 682.

VICTOR TERRAS

Detractors and Defenders
of Dostoevsky's Art

In his lifetime, Dostoevsky was not blessed with laudatory reviews. With time, he became defensive about the artistic quality of his work and made the excuse that he had had to write hurriedly, with no time to pay attention to stylistic niceties. Anybody familiar with Dostoevsky's notebooks, drafts, and galley proofs knows that this was hardly true. But generations of critics have used Dostoevsky's remarks to corroborate their negative assessment of his art.

Most negative opinions about Dostoevsky's art boil down to an assertion that, while his works are of some interest psychologically or philosophically, their artistic quality is low. Thus, N. A. Dobroliubov, in an otherwise positive review of Dostoevsky's novel *The Insulted and Injured*, "Downtrodden People" (*Zabitye liudi*, 1861), said in fact that it was "artistically below criticism." Some more recent critics, such as Ivan Bunin and Vladimir Nabokov, concur. To be sure, much negative criticism was and still is caused by the critics' disagreement with Dostoevsky's ideological positions or his general ethos ("good, but pretentious," said Chekhov).

As regards novelistic structure, some critics have seen Dostoevsky's plots as chaotic and disorganized, while others have found them "Gothic" and aimed at cheap effects. Still others have charged Dostoevsky with excessive psychologizing (his rival Turgenev found it intolerable) and with overly pronounced naturalism ("copying court records").[1] Many critics have found Dostoevsky's characters unrealistic, schematic, and contrived. The observation that they all talk alike—like the author—is heard often.

Even more intense is the criticism leveled at Dostoevsky's stylistic craftsmanship. From the very beginning, critics found his style prolix, repetitious, and lacking in polish. Often enough Dostoevsky was also found to be obscure, artificial, and sentimental. Finally, he has been found to lack balance, restraint, and good taste. In a word, whatever the merits of his oeuvre as a whole, its aesthetic value was found to be slight or nonexistent.

Great moral flaws have also been found in Dostoevsky's works. The charge heard most often is that of pessimism. Almost as often, the *outré*, hysterical, and morbid nature of Dostoevsky's works is held up to censure. The label of a "cruel talent" has stuck to him ever since N. K. Mikhailovsky's essay of that title (*Zhestokii talant*) appeared in 1882. Dostoevsky's fascination with the extremes of the human condition is condemned by many critics. Less common are charges of insincerity, unctuousness, and "rosy Christianity."[2]

The truth content of Dostoevsky's works has been often challenged as well. In particular, he is said to have pursued the exceptional instead of the typical. Tendentious distortion of reality is a common charge.[3] In an age of realism, Dostoevsky's penchant for the fantastic, the paradoxical, and the mystical met with much disapproval.[4]

These opinions, each voiced by critics of note, may be assumed to be representative of a substantial body of readers and deserve attention not only as a record of *Rezeptionsgeschichte*, but also as an avenue to an analysis of Dostoevsky's works.

As regards the structure of Dostoevsky's novels, the critics' dissatisfaction is well founded. If the ideal is a well spaced and, economically, developed linear plot, a Dostoevskian novel with its multitude of minor characters and subplots, inserted anecdotes, philosophical dialogues, and the narrator's essayistic and other digressions is hardly "well structured." It must be considered, though that this linear—or syntagmatic—view ignores the wealth of paradigmatic structures that may do quite as much to integrate the text as an elegant linear plot would: leitmotifs, situation rhyme, recurrent imagery, mirroring and doubling, symbolic foreshadowing, parallelism literary echoes and outright quotations, and other such devices are all plentiful in Dostoevsky's novels. Their effect tends to be subliminal, and their presence has been demonstrated only through the efforts of generations of literary scholars.[5]

Claims for Dostoevsky's greatness as a novelist must be staked in connection with the Bakhtinian sense of the novel as an all-inclusive, wide-open expression of the fullness of life in a world in flux. The pattern of a tightly structured tragic plot may be discerned within this loose texture.[6] Isaiah Berlin was, I believe, deeply wrong when he called Dostoevsky a monist "hedgehog" whose art is all about a single issue, rather than a "fox" with a bagful of tricks.[7] A great novelist in this Bakhtinian sense must be a pluralist. Dostoevsky is a pluralist in a variety of ways. He has been aptly called a "romantic realist."[8] He has been thought, certainly in the West, to be the most Russian of novelists; yet his greatest impact has been on Western readers. Dobroliubov considered Dostoevsky a champion of the "downtrodden," and his art is decidedly demotic, yet it came to be appreciated by the intellectual elite of the twentieth century, the Prousts, Gides, and Hermann Hesses.

All these contradictions are enhanced by what Bakhtin called the polyphonic quality of Dostoevsky's art: the presence in his texts of a persistent "other voice," generated by devices such as an ironic narrator, often himself the unwary butt of the implied author's irony, frequent "inner dialogue," multiple ambiguities, and an incessant stream of literary and journalistic quotations, echoes, and allusions.

Dostoevsky's texts contain many semantic levels. Their narrative level, itself many-faceted, is synchronized with a moral or political argument, such as the antinomy of human and divine justice in *The Brothers Karamazov*; an allegorical message, say, the prophetic anticipation of the Russian Revolution in *The Possessed*, and metaphysical symbolism, such as the theme of resurrection in *Crime and Punishment*.

Dostoevsky's novels encompass antagonistic philosophies and value systems. He is an excellent "devil's advocate." Sophisticated readers have mistaken for his own ideas what Dostoevsky was in fact trying to refute.[9] Dostoevsky's negative characters, his losers, scoundrels, and villains, are presented with as much empathy as his tragic heroes. Bakhtin drew attention to the carnivalistic strain in Dostoevsky's novels, where a tragic plot may develop from what was initially a scandalous incident or a bad joke. Burlesque comedy is interspersed with tragic action. Serious ideas are advanced by disreputable types, buffoons, or characters who are clearly wrong about things that are dear to the writer's heart. Often Dostoevsky's most cherished thoughts appear in travesty: Lebedev, a disreputable character, praying for the soul of the Countess Du Barry is in fact living up to Father Zosima's principle of universal guilt and responsibility.[10]

Dostoevsky's novels have been called ideological.[11] His heroes may be perceived as ideas incarnate and his plots as conflicts of ideas. But then, too, Dostoevsky "aimed at concreteness all his life," as Viktor Shklovsky put it.[12] A wealth of concrete detail, both incidental and significant, is to be found in his novels. Mundane concerns appear throughout in the most concrete terms. Dostoevsky is a master of the realistic *detail évocateur*. Sonia's plaid shawl, Stavrogin's little red spider, Arkady's white-and-blue checkered handkerchief, Iliusha's toy cannon, Aliosha's sausage sandwich, and hundreds of such details are remembered by the reader.

Dostoevsky's novels are ambiguous even structurally. On the one hand, they leave openings to "real life" in a variety of ways (including allusions to contemporary events and concerns, and especially to contemporary literature). On the other, they are structured artefacts by virtue of the presence in them of abstract ideas that are brought home through various artful devices. A tragic plot in which ancient mythical themes have been detected may be embedded in what is recognizably an old-fashioned family novel with many feuilletonistic digressions, as is the case in *The Idiot* and *The Brothers Karamazov*.

The charge that Dostoevsky's novels have Gothic traits and feature high or perverse passions, intrigue, murder, and suicide is of course valid. Dostoevsky's main characters are exceptional human beings in extreme situations. Yet it must be understood that they live in a world populated by crowds of ordinary people leading ordinary lives. The saints, fanatics, murderers, and tragic sufferers of Dostoevsky's novels live among men and women who pursue their mundane concerns in familiar ways. This does not invalidate the charge, however, and Dostoevsky's answer to it was that extreme types and situations were more revealing of the human condition than the so-called "average."[13] This is a fundamental question on which Dostoevsky disagreed with most of his contemporaries. Maximilian Braun has wisely suggested that the crises, rare but still real, of human life, were precisely Dostoevsky's forte, while he had less of an eye and ear for everyday life: courtship and marriage, making a living, raising a family, and such. Which area one considers more important depends on one's *Weltanschauung*.[14]

The charge of "naturalism" is also justified. This goes both for Dostoevsky's use of topics and details of current journalistic interest and for his frequent depictions of the seamy side of life and distasteful aspects of personal appearance and behavior. Dostoevsky offended not only Victorian sensibilities in this respect.[15]

As for Dostoevsky's characters, it is true that many of them are based on identifiable real-life prototypes. It is also true that these, as well as some other, apparently imaginary characters, are readily perceived as "types," which was Dostoevsky's intent. The portraits of, say, Turgenev in *The Possessed* or of G.Z. Eliseev in *The Brothers Karamazov* are indiscreetly recognizable and quite cruel. They are also drawn satirically, as social types. But this can hardly be considered an aesthetic blemish, unless one clings to a narrow conception of realist art that excludes satire on the grounds that it distorts reality.

More serious is M.E. Saltykov-Shchedrin's charge that *The Idiot* contains, "on the one side, characters full of life and truth, but on the other, some mysterious puppets whirling madly as though in a dream, made by hands trembling with rage."[16] Similar impressions come from other reputable critics who were at odds with Dostoevsky's political views. They tended to find Dostoevsky's characters contrived and carelessly executed. For instance, Mikhailovsky calls the nihilist figures in *The Possessed*, including Stavrogin, Piotr Verkhovensky, Shatov, and Kirillov, "puppets" and "pale, pretentious, and artificial."[17] Tolstoi's identical charge refers to *The Brothers Karamazov* as a whole.[18] These opinions are to be explained by the fact that the characters perceived as artificial, and contrived were in fact created as ideas incarnate. They owe their existence to the ideas that possess them.[19] Their social and psychological Gestalt is a function of these ideas. The disagreement between Dostoevsky and critics who would rather see ideas as a function of a character's social identity is of a basic nature. It is a disagreement between a positivist social determinism and Dostoevsky's idealist belief in the freedom of the human spirit.

Another violation of strict realism may be seen in Dostoevsky's tendency to give many of his characters the gift of imaginative expression. Too many of them talk and think well, or at least interestingly, to be altogether believable. Homer, Dante, and Shakespeare, to name only the greatest, take the same risk. The gain is in expressiveness. It is this form of poetic license that energizes Dostoevsky's texts and makes them so memorable.

The most damaging of the charges, that all Dostoevsky's characters talk like the author, has been heard often since V. G. Belinsky first leveled it, and from as authoritative a reader as Tolstoi.[20] It clashes with Bakhtin's polyphonic conception of the Dostoevskian novel.[21] How is this patent contradiction to be resolved? It is a fact that Dostoevsky, never a writer "from the notebook" (in the literal sense, that is), is not a very careful stylist when it comes to creating a social, regional, or occupational idiolect for his characters. He also lets some of his characters express thoughts which appear to be "over their heads" and which may be a part of the author's ideological argument. Furthermore, more than most novelists, Dostoevsky likes to introduce a literary subtext into his dialogue, a trait that runs the danger of deconstructing its realism, as the reader's mind is directed to the text quoted or alluded to and away from the situation at hand. The justification for this practice is that Dostoevsky's novels are not primarily novels of manners, or even realistic social novels, but are rather in many ways close to the tradition that began with the Platonic dialogue. They are novels about ideas as much about people.

Dostoevsky's texts are alive, rather than lucid, well written, or elegant. They present the narrator's and the characters' speech in living flux, rather than as a finished product. An undercurrent of emotion or thought-in-progress is constantly present. The text is energized by an ever-active "inner form," by which I mean any kind of verbal content beyond direct routine communication, or, in other words, any active ingredient added to the message by its medium. Metaphoric expression, such as *podpol'e*, "underground," *nadryv*, "rupture," or *besy*, "demons," is the most obvious example. "Inner form" may be generated also by rhythm, dialogic expression (as in irony, ambiguity, allusion, innuendo), over- and understatement, poignancy, solemnity, strangeness (through quirkiness, buffoonery, slang, idiolect, catachresis), challenging the reader by open partisanship, provocation, suspense, or novelty, and the narrator's and everybody else's unflagging personal interest in the action. "Inner form" makes the reader see things by making them concrete. For instance, the first chapter subtitle in *The Brothers Karamazov* might have been "The Story of a Family," which would have been routine communication without inner form. Instead, it is *Istoriia Odnoi Semeiki*—"The (Hi)Story of One Nice Little Family."

A reputation as a poor stylist has accompanied Dostoevsky since the publication of his first works. The critics' opinion is the result of a misunderstanding that has been removed by Bakhtin's insights. Bakhtin showed that Dostoevsky's text creates a polyphonic concert of living voices, one of which is the narrator's (which itself may well be dialogic!), rather than a homophonic narrative dominated by the narrator's voice. Hence a controlled, economical, and well-integrated narrative style is not what Dostoevsky pursues. He will write elegantly only when the voice in question demands it. If one disregards the "polyphony" argument, Dostoevsky's highly uneven narrative style, often distinctly colloquial, often journalistic, sometimes chatty, then again lyrical, solemn, or pathetic, places his work with the *roman-feuilleton* and may be legitimately seen as an aesthetic flaw. Today it is commonly seen as an innovative trait, adopted by Céline, Faulkner, Grass, and other leading novelists of the twentieth century.

The alleged moral flaws of Dostoevsky's works are a function of the critic's *Weltanschauung*. I believe that a Christian view close to Dostoevsky's lets these flaws disappear. This is also true of Dostoevsky's alleged pessimism. Thus, it is often said of *The Idiot* that the Good, personified in Prince Myshkin, is wholly ineffectual, and the ideal that the Prince stands for quite incompatible with life. Such criticism is invalid from Dostoevsky's Christian viewpoint, for a Christian's hope and joy are nurtured not by any earthly "and they lived happily ever after," but by faith in resurrection. A similar defense may be advanced against the charge that the atmosphere Dostoevsky created is sickly, hysterical, or *outré* (as he said himself). Nietzsche once called the evangelic world a mixture of the sickly, the childlike, and the sublime. The fervent excitement that permeates Dostoevsky's world is shared with every ambience of religious or political ferment.

Dostoevsky's religious thought is concerned with the ways in which men live and die *with* or *without* God. The solipsist antihero of *Notes from Underground*, the would-be Nietzschean *Übermensch* Raskolnikov, *l'homme revolté* Kirillov of *The Possessed*, burnt-out Byronic heroes like Svidrigailov and Stavrogin, sensualists like Fiodor Pavlovich

Karamazov, crude cynics like Smerdiakov, and even god-builders like
Ivan Karamazov or Versilov of *A Raw Youth*—they are all humanists who
believe that man can stand alone without God—or against God.
Dostoevsky's peculiar approach to existence without God made him a
forerunner of Existentialism. He asked not whether or not there is a
God, but what living with or without God means for the existence of
modern man.[22] Despite his efforts to discredit atheist humanism,
Dostoevsky became a prophet of the "death of God." He certainly
defined the condition of man without God with great power, though
this achievement may have lost some of its provocative edge in our
godless age.

Those of Dostoevsky's characters who are with God, holy men like
Tikhon, Makar Dolgoruky, or Zosima, simple souls like Sonia
Marmeladov, Prince Myshkin, or Aliosha Karamazov, humble sinners
like Marmeladov or Dmitry Karamazov, are no less memorable. Their
state of grace is not determined by good deeds, or even by the fruits of
their striving, but entirely by their unquestioning acceptance of God's
fatherhood. This position is complemented by a doctrine, stated most
clearly by Father Zosima, of human solidarity in sonhood, which lets
every human bear guilt and responsibility for every sin of humanity.[23]

Dostoevsky believed that a Christian's progress is a struggle *against*
human nature.[24] Man is sustained in this struggle by epiphanies of divine
grace, Father Zosima's "contacts with other worlds," which intrude upon
man's mundane existence. This position, and Dostoevsky's rejection of
ethical rationalism, are in accord not only with Orthodox doctrine, but
also with some strains of romantic idealism. Dostoevsky's religious
philosophy is generally in tune with Russian Slavophile thought.
Important as Dostoevsky's religious ideas and *Kulturkritik* may be, to see
his greatness mainly in these terms may divert us from an appreciation
of his genius, simply because today, as in the writer's lifetime, many
readers will reject these ideas out of hand.

As for the cruelty of Dostoevsky's talent, a charge raised by V. P.
Burenin[25] even before Mikhailovsky's celebrated article, and reiterated
by Nabokov, who speaks of Dostoevsky's "wallowing in the tragic
misadventures of human dignity," this too depends on the critic's point
of view. A remark by Saltykov-Shchedrin, rather to the same effect, may
put this trait in the right context. Speaking of *Notes from Underground*,
Saltykov-Shchedrin suggests that the point of this work is to show that

every man is trash; nor will he ever become a good man until he is convinced that he is indeed trash. He then adds: "In the end, he moves on to the real subject of his musings. He draws his proofs mostly from St. Thomas Aquinas, but since he fails to reveal this, his readers may think that these thoughts are the narrator's own."[26] The meaning of this Aesopian comment is that Dostoevsky has taken his hero to the depths of abjection only in order to lead him thereafter to faith and salvation. From a Christian viewpoint there is nothing wrong with this. But it is difficult for a reader who does not share Dostoevsky's Christian convictions to see it this way, or, for another example, to see Marmeladov, that image of abjection and degradation, as an edifying example and perhaps the most positive character of *Crime and Punishment*, discounting Sonia, who is a saint.

Other charges related to the moral aspect of Dostoevsky's works are also a matter of ideology. Such are the charges of unctuousness and "rosy Christianity." The former is a matter of faith: a nonbeliever like Nabokov will find the reading of the Gospel that brings together "the murderer and the harlot" to be simply in bad taste. The believer will find it moving and edifying. Leontiev's charge of "rosy Christianity," shared with some conservative Orthodox churchmen, may well be valid for some of Dostoevsky's writings, though not for his total oeuvre.

Turning now to the truth content of Dostoevsky's works, the foremost charge is that he deals with the exceptional, rather than with the typical: a serious charge, considering Dostoevsky's insistence that he was a realist, albeit "in a higher sense." V. G. Belinsky said that madmen—Dostoevsky's Goliadkin, hero of *The Double* (1846), is the case in point—being atypical, "belong in lunatic asylums, not in novels."[27] Dostoevsky, in commenting on his novel years later, said that he had heralded, precisely in this character, a new social type of importance. So Goliadkin's madness was typical after all. Analogous disagreements between author and critics were repeated in connection with almost every work. Dostoevsky was confident that the future would prove him right: his "exceptional" characters would one day be recognized as prophetic of Russia's future, while those of Goncharov, Turgenev, and Tolstoi would appear as what they were, even at their appearance: representations of Russia's past.[28] The last word may not yet have been said about Dostoevsky the prophet and religious thinker. His analysis of the mentality that caused the Russian Revolution was profoundly correct, yet he was wrong, judging from the present point in history, in assuming that Russian spirituality would prevail over the demons of godless humanism and nihilism.

The charges of outright distortion of reality relate mostly to Dostoevsky's understanding of the mood and moral attitude of the young generation of the Russian intelligentsia. It would seem that he was overly optimistic when he hoped that Kolia Krasotkin would follow the example of Aliosha Karamazov, rather than that of Rakitin.

Since the 1840s, Dostoevsky has had a reputation as a keen psychologist. Even then some critics found his psychologism excessive. In the 1860s and 1870s, such charges were heard frequently, and it was suggested that Dostoevsky's morbidly self-conscious and self-lacerating characters were unrepresentative of Russian society, but were, rather, projections of the author's own diseased mind. Unquestionably, Dostoevsky had a deep understanding of humans under conditions of great stress caused by want, suffering, frustration, rejection, and despair. He understood the psychology of poverty, humiliation, resentment, jealousy, cynicism, and cruelty better than most. Whether he had a balanced view of the Russian men and women of his age is a different question. Excellence as a psychologist is hardly the measure of his greatness, however, especially because Dostoevsky himself often spoke disparagingly of "scientific" psychology.[29]

As for the charge that Dostoevsky developed his psychological dramas in a vacuum, neglecting to give them a natural and social background, I believe that it is unfounded. A careful reader will find that each scene of a Dostoevskian novel is provided with ample and aptly chosen detail that acts as a proper setting for the scene. Some critics have said that mundane details, such as food and drink, clothing and land- or city-scape, are missing from Dostoevsky's novels. This is simply not true. There is ample material for an article on "Food and Drink in *The Brothers Karamazov*," for example, or on "The Topography of St. Petersburg in *Crime and Punishment*."

NOTES

1. P.N. Tkachev, "Bol'nye liudi," *Delo* 3/4 (1873). Quoted from F. M. Dostoevskii, *Polnoe sobranie sochinenii v tridtsati tomakh* (Leningrad: Nauka, 1972–90), 12:262. Hereafter abbreviated as *PSS*.

2. K.N. Leont'ev, "Nashi novye khristiane," *Sobranie sochinenii*, 9 vols. (Moscow, 1912), 8:183.

3. For example, N.K. Mikhailovskii, "Literaturnye i zhurnal'nye zametki," *Otechestvennye zapiski* (1873), no. 2/11, calls the nihilists of *The Possessed* "puppets."

4. M.A. Antonovich's review of *The Brothers Karamazov*, entitled "A Mystic-Ascetic Novel" (1881), concentrates on this issue.

5. Some key titles on these topics: Robert Belknap, *The Structure of* The Brothers Karamazov (The Hague: Mouton, 1967); Ralph E. Matlaw, "Recurrent Imagery in Dostoevskii," *Harvard Slavic Studies* 3:201–25; Dmitri Chizhevsky, "The Theme of the Double in Dostoevsky," in *Dostoevsky: A Collection of Critical Essays*, ed. René Wellek (Englewood Cliffs, N.J.: Prentice-Hall, 1962); Vyacheslav Ivanov, *Freedom and the Tragic Life: A Study of Dostoevsky*, trans. Norman Cameron (New York: Noonday, 1952); Nina Perlina, *Varieties of Poetic Utterance: Quotation in* The Brothers Karamazov (Lanham, Md.: University Presses of America, 1985).

6. See Chapter 5 for details.

7. Isaiah Berlin, *The Hedgehog and the Fox* (London: Weidenfeld & Nicolson, 1953).

8. Donald Fanger, *Dostoevsky and Romantic Realism: A Study of Dostoevsky in Relation to Balzac, Dickens and Gogol* (Cambridge: Harvard University Press, 1965).

9. This is particularly true of the Grand Inquisitor chapter of *The Brothers Karamazov*. V. V. Rozanov felt that Dostoevsky's attempts at a theodicy reflected his incapacity for true religious feeling: *Dostoevsky and the Legend of the Grand Inquisitor*, trans. Spencer E. Roberts (Ithaca: Cornell University Press, 1972), pp. 174–75, 189–90. Nikolai Berdiaev was not sure whose side Dostoevsky was on, God's or the Devil's: *Mirosozertsanie Dostoevskogo* (Prague: YMCA, 1923), p. 195. D.H. Lawrence found in the Grand Inquisitor chapter an irritating "cynical-satanical" pose, failing to realize that Dostoevsky had set up Ivan Karamazov in that pose: see Edward Wasiolek, *Dostoevsky: the Major Fiction* (Cambridge: MIT Press, 1964), p. 164.

10. L.P. Grossman has pointed out that Dostoevsky likes to develop high tragedy from what initially appears to be merely a scandalous occurrence. He is also fond of introducing strident dissonances; see my essay "Dissonance and False Notes in a Literary Text," in *The Structural Analysis of Narrative Texts* (Columbus: Slavica, 1980), pp. 82–95.

11. B.M. Engel'hardt, "Ideologicheskii roman Dostoevskogo," in *F. M. Dostoevskii: Stat'i i materialy*, ed. A. S. Dolinin (Moscow and Leningrad: Academia, 1924), 2:79–109.

12. Viktor Shklovskii, *Za i protiv: Zametki o Dostoevskom* (Moscow: Sovetskii pisatel', 1957), p. 15.

13. See the author's prefatory note in *The Brothers Karamazov*, PSS 14:5.

14. Maximilian Braun, *Dostojewskij: Das Gesamtwerk als Vielfalt und Einheit* (Göttingen: Vandenhoeck & Ruprecht, 1976), pp. 274–75.

15. This is a point emphasized by K.N. Leont'ev, "Novye Khristiane," who finds fault not only with Dostoevsky but also with Tolstoi for dwelling on characters' unaesthetic bodily functions.

16. M.E. Saltykov-Shchedrin, review of Omulevsky's novel *Shag za shagom*, *Otechestvennye zapiski* (1871): 300–308.

17. See Mikhailovskii, "Literaturnye i zhurnal'nye Zametki."

18. A.V. Chicherin, "Poeticheskii stroi iazyka v romanakh Dostoevskogo," in *Tvorchestvo F. M. Dostoevskogo* (Moscow: AN SSSR, 1959), draws attention to this passage in Tolstoi's diary (it refers to *The Brothers Karamazov*): "His dialogues are impossible and entirely unnatural.... I was surprised by his sloppiness, artificiality, the fabricated quality ... so awkward ... how unartistic: outright unartistic ... everybody speaking the same language" (p. 444).

19. Engel'hardt, "Ideologicheskii roman Dostoevskogo."

20. See n. 18 above.

21. M.M. Bakhtin, *Problemy tvorchestva Dostoevskogo* (Leningrad: Priboi, 1929).

22. For an analysis of this conception, see Ina Fuchs, "Homo Apostata," *die Entfremdung des Menschen: Philosophische Analysen zur Geistmetaphysik F.M. Dostojewskijs* (Munich: Otto Sagner, 1987).

23. PSS 14:290–92.

24. Stated clearly in the notebook passage *Masha lezhit na stole* ("Masha is laid out") of 1864, *PSS* 20:172–74.

25. V.P. Burenin's review of *The Possessed* in *Sankt-Peterburgskie vedomosti*, no. 250, October 11, 1871, quoted in *PSS* 12:260.

26. M.E. Saltykov-Shchedrin's feuilleton "Strizhi" (1864), quoted in *PSS* 5:312.

27. V.G. Belinskii, *Polnoe sobranie sochinenii*, 13 vols. (Moscow: AN SSSR, 1953–59), 10:41.

28. See notebooks for *The Possessed*, *PSS* 16:329.

29. See Chapter 3 for details.

MIKHAIL BAKHTIN

The Idea
in Dostoevsky's Works

Let us move on to the next element of our thesis—the statement of the idea in Dostoevsky's artistic world. The concept of polyphony is incompatible with the representation of a single idea (*odnoideinost'*) executed in the ordinary way. Dostoevsky's originality must be manifested with particular sharpness and clarity in the statement of the idea. In our analysis we shall avoid discussing the content of the ideas which Dostoevsky introduces—we are interested in their artistic function within the work.

The hero in Dostoevsky is not only a word about himself and about his immediate environment, but also a word about the world: he has not only a consciousness, but an ideology, too.

Already the "underground man" is an ideologist, although the ideological creativity of the heroes attains its full significance in the novels, where the idea does in fact almost become the heroine of the work. Nonetheless, the dominant of the hero's representation remains unchanged—it is the self-consciousness.

Therefore the hero's word about the world merges with his confessional word about himself. The truth about the world, according to Dostoevsky, is inseparable from the truth of the personality. The categories of self-consciousness which determined life already in the case of Devushkin, and especially in the case of Golyadkin,—acceptance or

From *Problems of Dostoevsky's Poetics* translated by R.W. Rotsel. © 1973 by Ardis. Reprinted by permission.

non-acceptance, revolt or meekness—in the novels become the basic
categories of thought about the world. Therefore the loftier principles
of *Weltanschauung* are the same as the principles of the most concrete
personal experience. Thus is achieved the artistic merging of personal
life with *Weltanschauung*, of intimate experience with the idea, which is
so characteristic of Dostoevsky. Personal life becomes uniquely unselfish
and principled, and lofty ideological thinking becomes intimately
personal and passionate.

The merging of the hero's word about himself with his ideological
word about the world greatly elevates the direct significance of his self-
utterance and strengthens his resistance to every external finalization.
The idea aids the self-consciousness in asserting its sovereignty within
Dostoevsky's artistic world and helps it triumph over every firm and
stable image.

But on the other hand the idea is able to retain its significance, its
full meaning, only when the self-consciousness is the dominant of the
hero's artistic representation. In a monological artistic world an idea,
placed in the mouth of a hero who is depicted as a firm and finalized
image of reality, inevitably loses its direct significance and becomes an
aspect, a predetermined feature of reality no different from any other of
the hero's traits. Such an idea is a social-typical or an individual-
characteristic one, or a mere intellectual gesture on the part of the hero,
the intellectual expression on his spiritual face. The idea ceases to be an
idea and becomes a simple artistic, characteristic. As such, it becomes a
part of the hero's image.

If an idea in a monological world retains its significance as an idea,
it is inevitably separated from the firm image of the hero and ceases to
be artistically combined with him: it is merely placed in his mouth, but
could with equal success be placed in the mouth of any other hero. The
author merely wants to be sure that a particular correct idea is expressed
in the context of a given work; who expresses it and when is determined
by the compositional considerations of convenience and
appropriateness, or on the basis of purely negative criteria: in such a way
that it does not destroy the speaker's verisimilitude. Such an idea *belongs
to no one*. The hero is a mere carrier of the independent idea; as a true,
significant idea, it gravitates toward a certain apersonal, systematic-
monological context, or in other words, toward the author's own
systematic-monological *Weltanschauung*.

The monological artistic world does not recognize the thoughts and ideas of others as an object of representation. In such a world everything ideological is divided into two categories. Certain thoughts—the true, significant ones—correspond to the author's consciousness and strive to take form in the purely semantic unity of the *Weltanschauung*; such thoughts are not represented, they are asserted; their assertion is objectively expressed in their special accent, their special position in the work as a whole, in the very verbal-stylistic form of their expression and by a whole series of other methods of advancing a confirmed, significant thought. We always detect such a thought in the context of the work; a confirmed thought has a different sound than an unconfirmed thought. The other ideas and thoughts—from the author's points of view incorrect or indifferent ones, ones which do not fit into his *Weltanschauung*—are not asserted, but rather are either polemically negated or lose their direct significance and become mere elements of characterization, the hero's intellectual gestures or his more permanent intellectual qualities.

In the monological world *tertium non datur*: a thought is either confirmed or negated; otherwise it simply ceases to be a thought of full significance. In order to become a part of the artistic structure, an unconfirmed thought must be deprived of its significance and become a psychic fact. Thoughts which are polemically negated are also not represented, because negation, in whatever form it may take, excludes the possibility of the genuine representation of an idea. A negated foreign thought (*otricaemaia chuzhaia mysl'*) does not break out of the monological context, but on the contrary, becomes the more harshly and implacably shut up within its own borders. A negated foreign thought is not capable of creating a full-fledged foreign consciousness side by side with another consciousness, so long as this negation remains the purely theoretical negation of a thought as such.

The artistic representation of an idea is possible only when it is stated in terms beyond confirmation and negation, but at the same time is not reduced to a mere psychological experience, devoid of direct significance. In a monological world such a statement of an idea is impossible: it contradicts the most basic principles of that world. Those basic principles go far beyond the bounds of art alone; they are the principles of the entire ideological culture of modern times. But what are those principles?

The principles of ideological monologism found their most striking and theoretically distinct expression in idealistic *philosophy*. In idealism the monistic principle, i.e. the assertion of the unity of *existence*, is transformed into the principle of the unity of the *consciousness*.

For us, of course, the important thing is not the philosophical side of the question, but rather a certain characteristic of ideology in general, a characteristic manifested in the idealistic transformation of the monism of existence into the monologism of consciousness. And this characteristic is, in turn, important for us only from the viewpoint of its further artistic application.

The unity of consciousness, which replaces the unity of existence, is inevitably transformed into the unity of a *single* consciousness; it makes no difference what metaphysical form it takes: "consciousness in general" ("*Bewusstsein überhaupt*"), "the absolute I," "the absolute spirit," "the normative consciousness," etc. Alongside this unified and inevitably *single* consciousness is to be found a multitude of empirical human consciousnesses. From the point of view of "consciousness in general" this plurality of consciousnesses is accidental and, so to speak, superfluous. Everything that is essential and true in those consciousnesses becomes part of the unified context of "consciousness in general" and is deprived of its individuality. That which is individual, that which distinguishes one consciousness from another one and from other ones, is unessential for cognition and falls within the sphere of the individual human being's psychic organization and limitation. From the point of view of truth, there are no individual consciousnesses. The only principle of the individualization of cognition recognized by idealism is error. Every correct judgement corresponds to a particular unified systematic-monological context, rather than being attached to a personality. Only error individualizes. Everything that is true finds a place for itself within the bounds of a single consciousness, and if it does not in fact find a place, it is for reasons incidental and extraneous to truth itself. Ideally a single consciousness and a single mouth are completely sufficient for total fullness of cognition; there is no need and no basis for a multitude of consciousnesses.

It should be pointed out that the inevitability of a single and unified consciousness by no means necessarily follows from the concept of the one and only truth (*edinaia istina*) itself. It is completely possible to imagine and to assume that this one and only truth requires a plurality of consciousnesses, and that it has, so to speak, the nature of an *event* and is born in the point of contact of various consciousnesses. Everything depends on one's conception of the truth and its relationship to the consciousness. The monological conception of cognition and truth is only one of the possible conceptions. It arises only where the consciousness is placed below existence and where the unity of existence is transformed into the unity of consciousness.

On the basis of philosophical monologism genuine interaction of consciousnesses is impossible, and therefore genuine dialog is also impossible. In essence, idealism knows only a single form of cognitive interaction between consciousnesses: he who knows and possesses the truth instructs him who errs and is ignorant of it, i.e. the interaction of teacher and pupil. Consequently only a pedagogical dialog is possible.[75]

The monological conception of the consciousness prevails in other spheres of ideological creative work as well. All that is significant and valuable is everywhere concentrated around a single center—the carrier. All idealistic creative work is thought of and perceived as a possible expression of a single consciousness, a single spirit. Even where the matter under discussion is a collective of a variety of creative forces, unity is still illustrated by the image of a single consciousness: the spirit of a nation, the spirit of a people, the spirit of history, etc. All that has significance can be collected in a single consciousness and subordinated to a unified accent; everything which is not amenable to such a reduction is accidental and unessential. In modern times European rationalism with its cult of unified and exclusive (*edinyi i edinstvennyi*) reason, and particularly the Enlightenment, during which the basic genres of European prose were formed, abetted the consolidation of the monological principle and its penetration into all spheres of ideological life. European utopism is also based on this monological principle. Utopian socialism with its faith in the omnipotence of convictions belongs here, too. Unity of meaning is everywhere represented by a single consciousness and a single point of view.

Faith in the self-sufficiency of a single consciousness in all spheres of ideological life is not a theory created by some thinker or other; no, it is a profound structural characteristic of the ideological creativity of modern times, the determinate of its inner and outer form. We can be interested here only in the literary manifestations of this characteristic.

The statement of an idea in literature is, as we have already seen, usually totally monologistical. An idea is either confirmed or negated. All confirmed ideas merge in the unified vision and representation of the author's consciousness; the unconfirmed ideas are distributed among the heroes and are no longer significant ideas, but social-typical or individually characteristic manifestations of thought. The primary knower, understander and seer is the author alone. Only he is an ideologist. The author's ideas are marked by the stamp of his own individuality. Thus *individuality and direct and valid ideological significance are combined* in the author *without detracting from each other*. But only in the author. In the heroes, individuality kills the significance of their ideas, or, if the significance of those ideas is retained, they are separated from the hero's individuality and combine with that of the author. Hence the work's *single ideological accent*; the appearance of a second accent is inevitably perceived as an inadmissable contradiction within the author's *Weltanschauung*.

A confirmed and full-valued authorial idea can perform a triple function in a monological work: firstly, it is the *principle of the vision and representation of the world*, the principle of the *choice* and unification of material, the principle of the *ideological singletonedness* of all elements of the work. Secondly, the idea can be given as a more or less distinct or conscious *conclusion* drawn from that which is being represented. Thirdly, the author's idea can be given direct expression in the *ideological position of the central hero*.

The idea as a principle of representation becomes one with the form. It determines all the formal accents and all the ideological assessments which constitute the formal unity of artistic style and the unified tone of the work.

The deeper strata of this form-determining ideology, the factors which determine the basic characteristics of a work's genre, are of a traditional nature, they take shape and develop over the course of centuries. Artistic monologism belongs to this realm of the deeper strata of form.

Within a monological framework, ideology seen as a conclusion, as a summation of the meaning of that which is represented, inevitably transforms the represented world into the *voiceless object of that conclusion*. The forms of the ideological conclusion themselves can be most varied. The statement of the represented material depends upon those forms: the material can be the simple illustration of an idea, a mere example; it can be the basis for an ideological generalization (the experimental novel); or, finally, it can have a more complex relationship to the final sum. If the representation is oriented entirely toward an ideological conclusion, the result is an ideological, philosophical novel (Voltaire's *Candide*, for example), or—at worst—simply a crudely tendentious novel. And even if this direct orientation is absent, an element of ideological conclusion is nonetheless present in every representation, however modest or concealed the formal functions of that conclusion may be. The accents of the ideological conclusion must not contradict the form-determining accents of the representation itself. If such a contradiction exists, it is perceived as a shortcoming, for within a monological world contradictory accents collide in a single voice. Unity of viewpoint must weld together the most formal elements of style as well as the most abstract philosophical conclusions.

The hero's philosophical position can lie in the same plane as the form-determining ideology and the final ideological conclusion. The hero's point of view can be transferred from the objective sphere to the sphere of principle. In that case the ideological principles which lie at the basis of the structure no longer depict only the hero and determine the author's point of view toward him; those principles are now also expressed by the hero himself and determine his own point of view toward the world. Such a hero is formally very different from the ordinary type of hero. It is not necessary to go beyond the bounds of a given work to find other documentation of the concurrence of the author's ideology with that of the hero. Moreover, such a concurrence of content, having no basis in the work, is in itself possessed of no power to convince. The unity of the author's ideological principles of representation and the hero's ideological position must be revealed in the work itself, as the *single-accentedness of the representation and the speeches and experiences of the hero*, rather than as the concurrence of the hero's thoughts with the ideological views of the author, as stated in some other place. The very words and experiences of such a hero are presented differently: they are not materialized, they characterize not only the speaker himself, but the object at which they are directed as well. Such a hero's word lies in the same plane as the author's word.

The absence of distance, between the position of the author and that of the hero is manifested in a whole series of other formal characteristics as well. The hero, for example, is, like the author himself, not closed and inwardly finalized, and therefore does not fit wholly into the Procrustian bed of the plot, which is thought of as only one of many possible plots, and is consequently for the given hero an accidental one. This open-ended hero is typical of the Romanticists, of Byron and Chateaubriand; Lermontov's Pechorin is in some ways such a hero.

And finally, the author's ideas can be sporadically scattered throughout the entire work. They can appear in the author's speeches as isolated apothegms, maxims, or entire discourses, or they can be put into the mouth of one or another hero, sometimes in large quantities, without, however, merging with his individuality (Turgenev's Potugin, for example).

This whole mass of organized and unorganized ideology, from the principles which determine the form, to the chance and easily ignored maxims of the author, must be subordinated to a single accent and must express a single and unified point of view. Everything that remains is the object of this point of view, i.e. is subordinated to the accent. Only ideas which fall into the groove of the author's point of view can retain their significance without destroying the single-accented unity of the work. *None* of these authorial ideas, regardless of their function, are *represented*; they either represent and internally direct the representation, or they shed light on that which is represented, or, finally, they accompany the representation as separable semantic ornaments (*otdelimyi smyslovoi ornament*). *They are expressed directly, without distance.* And within the bounds of the monological world which they represent, a foreign idea cannot be represented. It is either assimilated or polemically refuted, or ceases to be an idea altogether.

Dostoevsky was capable of *representing a foreign (chuzhaia) idea*, while still maintaining its full meaning as an idea, and at the same time maintaining distance as well, not confirming the idea and not merging it with his own expressed ideology.

In his work the idea becomes an *object of artistic representation*, and Dostoevsky himself became a great *artist of the idea.*

It is characteristic that the image of an artist of the idea occurred to Dostoevsky already in 1846–47, i.e. at the very beginning of his creative path. We have in mind the image of Ordynov, the hero of "The Landlady." He is a lonesome young scholar. He has his own creative system, his own unusual approach to the scientific idea:

He was creating a system for himself; it grew within him over a period of years, and in his soul a still vague and obscure, but somehow wonderfully joyful *image of an idea* was gradually taking shape, an idea embodied in a *new, blissful form*, and that form struggled to burst out of his soul, tearing at it and tormenting it; he still timidly *sensed* its originality, its *truth* and its uniqueness: creativity was already revealing itself to his powers; it was taking form and gaining strength (I, 425).

And at the end of the story:

Perhaps a complete, original, unique idea would have been born in him. Perhaps he was destined to become an *artist in science*. (I, 498)

Dostoevsky was also destined to become an artist of the idea, not in science, but in literature.

What are the conditions which make the artistic representation of an idea possible for Dostoevsky?

First of all we must be reminded that the image of the idea is inseparable from the image of the person, the carrier of that idea. It is not the idea in and of itself which is the "heroine of Dostoevsky's works," as B.M. Engelgardt asserts, but rather the *man of an idea* (*chelovek idei*). We must again emphasize that Dostoevsky's hero is the man of an idea; this is not a character or temperament, not a social or psychological type: the image of a *full-valued* idea has, of course, nothing to do with such externalized and finalized images of people. It would, for example, be foolish to even attempt to combine Raskolnikov's idea, which we understand and *feel* (according to Dostoevsky an idea can and must be not only understood, but "felt" as well), with his finalized character or his social typicality as a *raznochinec* of the '60's: his idea would immediately lose its direct significance as a full-valued idea and would be removed from the conflict in which it lives in ceaseless dialogical interaction with other full-valued ideas—those of Sonya, Porfiry, Svidrigailov, etc. The carrier of a full-valued idea can be none other than the "man in man," with his free unfinalizedness and indeterminacy, about whom we spoke in the previous chapter. It is precisely to this unfinalized inner nucleus of Raskolnikov's personality that Sonya, Porfiry and others dialogically address themselves. It is also to this unfinalized nucleus of Raskolnikov's personality that the author, by virtue of the whole structure of his novel, addresses himself.

Consequently only the unfinalizable and inexhaustible "man in man" can become the man of an idea, whose image is combined with the image of a full-valued idea. This is the first condition of the representation of the idea in Dostoevsky.

But this condition contains, as it were, its inverse as well. We can say that in Dostoevsky's works man overcomes his "thingness" (*veshchnost'*) and becomes "man in man" only by entering the pure and unfinalized sphere of the idea, i.e. only by becoming the selfless man of an idea. Such are all of Dostoevsky's leading characters, i.e. all of the participants in the great dialog.

In this respect Zosima's definition of Ivan Karamazov's personality is applicable to all of these characters. Zosima of course couched his definition in his theological language, i.e. it stemmed from that sphere of the Christian idea in which he lived. We shall quote the appropriate passage from that—for Dostoevsky—very characteristic *penetrant* (*proniknovennyi*) dialog between the Elder Zosima and Ivan Karamazov.

> "Is that really your conviction regarding the consequences of the withering of people's faith in the immortality of their souls?" the Elder Zosima asked Ivan suddenly.
>
> "Yes, I have asserted that. If there is no immortality; there is no virtue."
>
> "You are blissfully happy if you really believe that. Or terribly unhappy."
>
> "Why unhappy?" smiled Ivan.
>
> "Because in all probability you do not yourself believe either in the immortality of your soul, nor in the things that you have written about the church and the religious question."
>
> "Perhaps you are right! ... But nonetheless it was not all merely a jest ...," suddenly admitted Ivan strangely, blushing quickly, by the way.
>
> "Verily, it was not all merely a jest. *This idea is not yet resolved in your heart, and it torments you.* But he who is

tormented is also fond at times of amusing himself with his despair, as if also out of despair. For the time being you, too, are amusing yourself with your despair—and with newspaper articles and worldly arguments, without yourself believing in your dialectic, under your breath laughing at it with pain in your heart ... *This question is unresolved in you, and that is your great misfortune, for it persistently demands a resolution ...*"

"But perhaps it is already resolved? Resolved in a positive direction?" Ivan continued to ask strangely, gazing steadily at the elder with some sort of inexplicable smile.

"If it cannot be resolved in a positive direction, it will never be resolved in a negative one, either; you yourself know this characteristic of your heart. Therein lies all its torment. But thank the Creator for giving you an *extraordinary heart, a heart capable of suffering such sufferings,* of '*setting its mind on things above, not on things on the earth, seeking those things which are above,* for our home is in the kingdom of heaven.' May God grant that the resolution of your heart come while you are still on earth, and may God bless your path!" (IX, 91–92)

In his discussion with Rakitin Alyosha defines Ivan similarly, only in more worldly language:

"Ach, Misha, his soul [Ivan's—M.B.] is a stormy one. His mind is held captive. He is filled with a great and unresolved idea: *He is one of those who don't need millions, they just need to get an idea straight.*" (IX, 105)

All of Dostoevsky's leading characters have the capacity to "set their minds on things above" and to "seek those things which are above;" each of them is filled with a "great and unresolved idea," all of them must above all "get an idea straight." And in this resolution of an idea lies their entire real life and their personal unfinalizedness. If one were to think away the idea in which they live, their image would be totally destroyed. In other words, the image of the hero is inseparably linked with the image of the idea. We *see* the hero in and through the idea, and we *see* the idea in and through the hero.

All of Dostoevsky's leading characters, as people of an idea, are absolutely unselfish, in so far as the idea has in fact taken command of the deepest core of their personality. This unselfishness is not a trait of their objective character and not an external description of their actions; unselfishness expresses their real life in the sphere of the idea (they "don't need millions, they just need to get an idea straight"). Living an idea (*ideinost'*) is somehow synonymous with unselfishness. In this sense even Raskolnikov is absolutely unselfish when he kills and robs the old woman usurer, as is the prostitute Sonya and the accomplice in the murder of Ivan Karamazov's father; the "raw youth's" *idea* to become a Rothschild is also absolutely unselfish. We repeat again: the important thing is not the ordinary classification of a person's character and actions, but rather the indicator of the dedication of his whole personality to the idea.

The second condition for the creation of the image of the idea in Dostoevsky is his profound understanding of the dialogical nature of human thought, the dialogical nature of the idea. Dostoevsky was able to see, reveal and depict the true sphere of the life of an idea. An idea does not live in one person's *isolated* individual consciousness—if it remains there it degenerates and dies. An idea begins to live, i.e. to take shape, to develop, to find and renew its verbal expression, and to give birth to new ideas only when it enters into genuine dialogical relationships with other, *foreign*, ideas. Human thought becomes genuine thought, i.e. an idea, only under the conditions of a living contact with another foreign thought, embodied in the voice of another person, that is, in the consciousness of another person as expressed in his word. It is in the point of contact of these voice-consciousnesses that the idea is born and has its life.

The idea, as *seen* by Dostoevsky the artist, is not a subjective individual-psychological formulation with a "permanent residence" in a person's head; no, the idea is interindividual and intersubjective. The sphere of its existence is not the individual consciousness, but the dialogical intercourse *between* consciousnesses. The idea is a *living event* which is played out in the point where two or more consciousnesses meet dialogically. In this respect the idea resembles the word, with which it forms a dialogical unity. Like the word, the idea wants to be heard, understood and "answered" by other voices from other positions. Like the word, the idea is by nature dialogical, the monolog being merely the conventional form of its expression which arose from the soil of the ideological monologism of modern times, as characterized above.

Dostoevsky saw and artistically represented the *idea* as precisely such a living event, played out between consciousness-voices. The artistic revelation of the dialogical nature of the idea, the consciousness, and of every human life that is illuminated by a consciousness (and therefore is at least marginally acquainted with ideas) made Dostoevsky a great artist of the idea.

Dostoevsky never sets forth completed ideas in monological form, but neither does he depict their psychological evolution within a *single* individual consciousness. In both cases the ideas would cease to be living images.

We recall, for example, Raskolnikov's first interior monolog, which we quoted in the preceding chapter. Here we find no psychological evolution of the idea within a *single* self-enclosed consciousness. On the contrary, the consciousness of the solitary Raskolnikov becomes the field of battle for the voices of others; the events of recent days (his mother's letter, the meeting with Marmeladov), reflected in his consciousness, take on the form of an intense dialog with absentee interlocutors (with his sister, his mother, Sonya, and others), and in this dialog, he, too, seeks to "get his ideas straight."

Already before the action of the novel begins, Raskolnikov has published a newspaper article containing an exposition of the theoretical bases of his idea. Dostoevsky nowhere gives us this article in monological form. We first become acquainted with its content, and consequently with Raskolnikov's main idea, in Raskolnikov's tense and, for him, terrible, dialog with Porfiry (Razumikhin and Zametov also participate in the dialog). Porfiry is the first to give an account of the article, and he does so in a deliberately exaggerated and provocative form. This internally dialogized account is constantly interrupted by questions put to Raskolnikov, and by the replies of the latter. Then Raskolnikov himself describes his article, but he is constantly interrupted by Porfiry's provocative questions and remarks. And, from the point of view of Porfiry and his like, Raskolnikov's account is saturated with inner polemics. Razumikhin also gives his comments. As a result, Raskolnikov's idea appears before us in the interindividual zone of intense struggle between several individual consciousnesses, while the idea's theoretical side is indissolubly combined in the ultimate life-principles of the dialog's participants.

This same idea of Raskolnikov appears again in his no less tense dialogs with Sonya; here it takes on a different tonality, entering into dialogical contact with another very strong and integral life-principle, that of Sonya, thus revealing new facets and potentialities: Next we hear this idea in Svidrigailov's dialogized presentation in his conversation with Dunya. But in the voice of Svidrigailov, who is one of Raskolnikov's parodical doubles, the idea has a completely different sound, and it turns another of its sides toward us. And lastly, Raskolnikov's idea comes into contact throughout the entire novel with various manifestations of life, it is tried and tested, and it is confirmed or refuted by them. This aspect was discussed in the preceding chapter.

Let us also recall Ivan Karamazov's idea that "everything is permissible" ("*vse pozvoleno*") as long as the soul is not immortal. What an intense dialogical life this idea lives throughout the entire novel *The Brothers Karamazov*! What a variety of voices expresses it and what unexpected dialogical contacts it makes!

Both of these ideas (Raskolnikov's and Ivan Karamazov's) reflect other ideas, just as in painting a certain color, because of the reflections of the surrounding colors, loses its abstract purity, but in return begins to live a truly colorful life. If one were to withdraw these ideas from the dialogical sphere of their lives and give them a monologically completed theoretical form, what cachetic and easily-refuted ideological constructions would result!

As an artist Dostoevsky did not create his ideas in the same way that philosophers and scholars create theirs—he created living images of the ideas which he found, detected, or sometimes divined in *reality itself,* i.e. images of already living ideas, ideas already existing as idea-forces. Dostoevsky possessed a brilliant gift for hearing the dialog of his age, or, more precisely, for perceiving his age as a great dialog, and for capturing in it not only individual voices, but above all the *dialogical relationships* between voices, their dialogical *interaction*. He heard both the dominant, recognized, loud voices of the age, that is to say, the dominant, leading ideas (both official and unofficial), and the still-weak voices, the ideas which had not yet reached full development, the latent ideas which no one else had yet discerned, and the ideas which were only beginning to mature, the embryos of future *Weltanschauungen*. Dostoevsky himself wrote: "Reality is not limited to the familiar, the commonplace, for it consists in huge part of a *latent, as yet unspoken future Word*."[76]

In the dialog of his times Dostoevsky heard the resonances of the voice—ideas of the past, too—both of the recent past (the 1830s and 40s), and of the more remote. He also strove, as we have just said, to discern the voice-ideas of the future, seeking to divine them, so to speak, in the place prepared for them in the dialog of the present, in the same way that it is possible to foresee a reply which has not yet been uttered in a dialog which is already in progress. Thus the past, the present, and the future came together and confronted one another in the plane of contemporaneity.

We repeat: Dostoevsky never created his idea-images out of nothing, he never "invented" them, any more than a painter invents the people he paints; he was able to hear and divine them in existing reality. Therefore it is possible to find and point out the specific *prototypes* of the ideas in Dostoevsky's novels, as well as those of his heroes. The prototypes of Raskolnikov's ideas, for example, were the ideas of Max Stirner as expressed in his tract "Der Einzige und sein Eigentum," and the ideas of Napoleon III, developed in his book *Histoire de Jules César* (1865);[77] one of the prototypes for Petr Verkhovensky's ideas was *Catechism of a Revolutionary*;[78] the prototypes of Versilov's ideas (in *A Raw Youth*) were the ideas of Chaadaev and Herzen.[79] Not all of the prototypes for Dostoevsky's idea-images have as yet been discovered. We must emphasize that we are not referring here to Dostoevsky's "sources"—that term would be inappropriate—but precisely to the *prototypes* of his images of ideas.

Dostoevsky in no way copied or expounded on these prototypes; he freely and creatively re-worked them into living artistic images of ideas, in the very same way that an artist works with his human prototypes. Above all, he destroyed the self-enclosed monological form of his idea-prototypes and made them part of the great dialog of his novels, where they begin to live a new, eventful artistic life.

As an artist, Dostoevsky revealed in the image of a given idea not only the actual and historical traits which were present in the prototype (in Napoleon's *Histoire de Jules César*, for example), but its *potentialities* as well, and it is just these potentialities that are of prime importance for an artistic image. Dostoevsky often made artistic conjectures as to how a given idea would develop and behave under certain altered conditions, or as to the unexpected directions its further development and transformation would take. For this purpose Dostoevsky placed the idea at the vertex of dialogically intersecting consciousnesses. He brought together ideas and *Weltanschauungen* which were in real life completely divergent and deaf to one another, and caused them to dispute. He as it were extended these ideas by means of a dotted line to their point of intersection. Thus he anticipated the future convergence of ideas which were as yet divergent. He foresaw new combinations of ideas, the emergence of new idea-voices, and changes in the arrangement of all the idea-voices in the universal dialog. This is why the Russian—and universal—dialog of Dostoevsky's works, a dialog of already-living idea-voices with idea-voices that are still being born, that are still unfinalized and fraught with new possibilities, continues to involve the minds and voices of Dostoevsky's readers in its tragic and exalted game.

Thus the idea-prototypes used in Dostoevsky's novels alter the form of their existence, without losing the significance of their meaning: they become completely dialogized, not monologically finalized, images of ideas, i.e. they enter a new sphere of *artistic* existence.

Dostoevsky was not only an artist who wrote novels and stories, but also a publicist-thinker who published articles in *Vremia, Epoxa, Grazhdanin* and *Dnevnik pisatelia* (*Time, The Epoch, The Citizen* and *Diary of a Writer*). In those articles he expressed specific philosophical, religious-philosophical, social-political, and other ideas; in the articles he expressed *his own confirmed* ideas in *systematic-monological* or rhetorical-monological (i.e. *publicistic*) form. He sometimes expressed the same ideas in letters to various people. Here, in the articles and letters, he give, of course, not images of ideas, but direct, monologically confirmed ideas.

But we meet these "Dostoevskian ideas" in his novels as well. How should we regard them there, i.e. in the artistic context of his creative work?

In exactly the same way as we regard Napoleon III's ideas in *Crime and Punishment* (ideas with which Dostoevsky the thinker was totally at variance), or the ideas of Chaadaev and Herzen in *A Raw Youth* (ideas with which Dostoevsky the thinker was in partial agreement); i.e. we should regard the ideas of Dostoevsky the thinker as *idea-prototypes* for certain idea-images in his novels (the images of the ideas of Sonya, Myshkin, Alyosha Karamazov, Zosima).

Actually, the ideas of Dostoevsky the thinker change the very form of their existence when they become part of his polyphonic novel; they are turned into artistic images of ideas: they become indissoluably combined with the images of people (Sonya, Myshkin, Zosima), they are freed from their monological isolation and finalization, becoming completely dialogized and entering into the great dialog of the novel *on completely equal terms* with other idea-images (the ideas of Raskolnikov, Ivan Karamazov and others). It is totally inadmissable to ascribe to them the finalizing function of the author's ideas in a monological novel. As equal participants in the great dialog, they simply do not have such a function. If a certain partiality of Dostoevsky the publicist for various ideas or images is sometimes felt in the novels, it is manifested only in superficial ways (as in the conventional-monological epilogue to *Crime and Punishment*, for example) and cannot destroy the powerful artistic logic of the polyphonic novel. Dostoevsky the artist always wins out over Dostoevsky the publicist.

Thus Dostoevsky's private ideas, expressed in monological form outside the artistic context for his work (in articles, letters and conversations), are only the prototypes of certain images of ideas in his novels. For this reason it is to tally inadmissable to substitute a criticism of these monological idea-prototypes for a genuine analysis of Dostoevsky's polyphonic artistic thought. It is important that the *function* of ideas in Dostoevsky's polyphonic world be revealed, and not only their *monological substance*.

For a correct understanding of the representation of the idea in Dostoevsky's works it is imperative to consider one more characteristic of the ideology which determined their form. We have in mind above all that ideology which was the principle of Dostoevsky's vision and representation of the world, the ideology which indeed determined the form of his works, because it is what, in the final analysis, determines the function of abstract ideas and thoughts in those works. The two basic elements on which any ideology is founded were absent from Dostoevsky's form-determining ideology: the *individual thought* and a unified *system* of thoughts in relation to the subject matter. An ordinary ideology contains separate thoughts, assertions and propositions which of themselves can be either correct or incorrect, depending on their relationship to the subject matter, and regardless of who is their carrier, regardless of whom they belong to. These "no-man's" thoughts, correct in relation to the subject matter (*"nich'i" predmetnovernye mysli*), are unified in the subject matter's systematic oneness. In the unity of the system, thought brushes against thought and one thought is bound to another on the basis of the subject matter. For the thought, the system is the ultimate whole, and the elements which form the system are the individual thoughts.

In this sense Dostoevsky's ideology contains neither the separate thought, nor a systematic unity. For him the basic, indivisible unit was not the individual thought, proposition or assertion, based on and limited to the subject matter (*predmetno-ogranichenaia*), but rather the integrated point of view, the integrated position of a personality. For him subject-oriented meaning is inseparably combined with the position of the personality. The personality presents itself full-blown in every thought. Therefore the combining of thoughts is the combining of integrated positions, the combining of personalities.

To speak paradoxically, Dostoevsky thought not in thoughts, but in points of view, in consciousnesses, in voices. He strove to perceive and formulate every thought in such a way that the whole man could express himself and resonate within it, thus expressing in compressed form his entire *Weltanschauung*, from alpha to omega. Only thoughts which squeezed an entire spiritual orientation into themselves were taken by Dostoevsky as elements of his artistic *Weltanschauung*; such thoughts were for him indivisible units, and such units combined to form a concrete event of organized human orientations and voices, not merely a unified system based on the subject matter. In Dostoevsky's works two thoughts are already two people, for there are no no-man's thoughts— every thought represents a whole person.

Dostoevsky's effort to perceive every thought as an integrated personal position and to think in voices can be clearly seen even in the composition of his publicistic articles. His manner of developing a thought is everywhere the same: he develops its dialogically, not in a dry logical dialog, but by juxtaposing deeply individualized integral voices. Even in his polemical articles he essentially does not try to persuade; rather he organizes voices and couples philosophical orientations, in most cases in the form of an imagined dialog.

Here is the typical structure of one of his articles.

In the article "Sreda" ("The Environment") Dostoevsky begins by stating a series of propositions in the form of questions and assumptions about the psychological state and orientation of jury members, interrupting and illustrating his thoughts, as usual, with the voices and semi-voices of individuals; for example:

> It would seem that one of the feelings (among others, of course) common to all jury members in the world, but to ours in particular, is the feeling of power, or, to put it better, the feeling of absolute might. This is sometimes an obscene feeling, i.e. when it dominates all others... In my daydreams I have imagined court sessions in which almost all of the jurors are, for example, peasants, who were only yesterday serfs. The prosecutor and the attorneys for the defense appeal to them and curry their favor and glance at them, but our old peasants sit there and say to themselves: "Well, now then, if I want to, I'll let 'em go, and if I don't—off to Siberia with 'em ..."
>
> Others will decide, as we have sometimes heard, "It's a pity to ruin somebody's life; they're people, too, after all. The Russian folk is merciful ..."

Further on Dostoevsky orchestrates his theme with the aid of an imaginary dialog.

> I hear a voice saying, "Even if we assume that those weighty principles of yours (i.e. Christian ones) are still the same and that it is true that one must be a citizen first of all, and hold up the flag, as you said, and so on; even if we assume so for now without an argument, just think, where are our citizens supposed to come from? Just imagine what things were like only yesterday! All these civil rights (and what generous ones, at that!) have suddenly come crashing down on the peasant like an avalanche. They've crushed him, they're as yet nothing but a burden for him, a burden!"
>
> "Of course there is justice in what you say," I answer the voice, hanging my head a bit, "but still, the Russian folk ..."
>
> "The Russian folk? If you please," I hear another voice

speaking, "someone says that gifts came crashing down on the peasant like an avalanche and crushed him. But maybe he feels not only that he received so much power as a gift, but beyond that maybe he feels that he got it for nothing, that is, that he is not yet worthy of these gifts ..." (This point of view is then developed further.)

"This is in part a slavophile voice," I think to myself. This thought is indeed comforting, and the conjecture about the peasant's meekness before the power which he has received as a gift, and of which he is not yet 'worthy' is certainly more charitable than the conjecture about his desire to make fun of the public prosecutor ..." (Development of the answer.).

"Well, see here," says a caustic voice, "you seem to be forcing some new-fangled philosophy of environment on the peasantry, but where does that come from? Sometimes all twelve of these jurors are peasants, and every last one of them thinks it's a mortal sin to eat the forbidden foods during Lent. And you want to go accusing them of social tendencies."

"Of course, of course, how should they have any idea about the 'environment,' that is, the whole lot of them," I think to myself, "but still, there are ideas in the air, and ideas have something penetrating about them ..."

"Well I never," laughs the caustic voice.

"And what if our peasantry is particularly inclined to the doctrine of the environment, by nature, perhaps, or because of its Slavic tendencies? What if the Russian folk is the most favorable material in all of Europe for the propagandists?"

The caustic voice laughs louder yet, but it is somehow not convincing.[80]

This theme is further developed by means of semi-voices and with concrete, everyday scenes and situations, each having as its final goal the characterization of some human orientation or another: that of the criminal, the lawyer, the juror, etc.

Many of Dostoevsky's publicistic articles are constructed in this way. His thought always finds its way through the labyrinth of voices and semi-voices and the words and gestures of other people. He never proves his propositions on the material of other abstract propositions, nor does he combine thoughts according to subject matter, but instead juxtaposes orientations and among them builds his own orientation.

Of course in such articles the form-determining characteristic of Dostoevsky's ideology is not able to manifest itself with sufficient depth. In the articles it is simply the form of the exposition, and the monological mode of thinking is not overcome. Publicistics offers the least favorable conditions for overcoming monologism. Nonetheless, Dostoevsky here, too, is not able, and does not want, to separate the thought from the man and his living lips in order to bind it to another thought in a purely objective (*predmetnyi*), impersonal plane. While the usual ideological orientation sees the objective sense, the objective "treetops" in an idea, Dostoevsky sees above all its "roots" in man; for him an idea has two sides, and these two sides, according to Dostoevsky, cannot be even abstractly separated. His entire material unfolds before him as a series of human orientations. His path leads not from idea to idea, but from orientation to orientation. For him, to think means to question and to listen, to try out orientations, incorporating same and unmasking others. It should be emphasized that in Dostoevsky's world even *agreement* (*soglasie*) retains its *dialogical* character, i.e. it never leads to a *merging* of voices and truths in a single *impersonal* truth, as is the case in the monological world.

It is characteristic that Dostoevsky's works are completely devoid of *separate* ideas, propositions and formulations, such as maxims, apothegms and aphorisms, which, when removed from their context and separated from their voice, retain their significance in an impersonal form. But how many such separate, true thoughts can be (and usually are) culled from the novels of L. Tolstoy, Turgenev, Balzac, etc., where they are sprinkled throughout the speeches of the characters and in the author's speech; separated from their voice, they retain their entire impersonal aphoristic significance.

In the literature of classicism and of the Enlightenment there developed a special aphoristic way of thinking, i.e. thinking in separate well-rounded and self-sufficient thoughts which were purposely independent of their context. The Romanticists developed another type of aphoristic thinking.

Such forms of thinking were particularly foreign and antagonistic to Dostoevsky. His form-determining *Weltanschauung* recognizes no *impersonal truth*, and in his works there are no detached, impersonal verities. There are only integral, indivisible idea-voices or viewpoint-voices, but they, too, cannot be detached from the dialogical fabric of the work without distorting their nature.

True, there are among Dostoevsky's characters representatives of the worldly, epigonic style of aphoristic thinking, or, rather, aphoristic babbling, who, like old prince Sokolsky (in *A Raw Youth*) spout banal witticisms and aphorisms. To their number belongs Versilov, but only partly, only because of a peripheral side of his personality. These worldly aphorisms are, of course, objectivized. But there is a special type of hero in Dostoevsky's works—Stepan Trofimovich Verkhovensky. He is an epigone of a higher style of aphoristic thinking—the enlightened and romantic. He spouts his "verities" because he lacks a "dominant idea" which would determine the core of his personality; he possesses separate impersonal verities which because of their impersonality, cease to be completely true, but he lacks a truth of his own. In the hours before his death he defines his own relationship to the truth:

> "My friend, I've been a liar all my life. Even when I spoke the truth. I never spoke for truth's sake, only for my own; I used to know it, but only now do I see ..." (VI, 678)

Out of context none of Stepan Trofimovich's aphorisms retains its full meaning, they are to a certain degree objectivized, and they are stamped with the author's irony (i.e. they are double-voiced).

There are also no separate thoughts or propositions in the dialogs of Dostoevsky's characters which take place within the composition of his works. They always argue on the basis of *integrated points of view*, rather than over *separate points*; they put themselves and their whole idea body and soul into even the shortest speech. They almost never take apart and analyze their integrated ideological positions.

Also in the great dialog of the novel the separate voices and their worlds are counterposed as inseparable wholes, rather than being broken down into separate points and propositions.

Dostoevsky very aptly characterizes his method of integral dialogical contrapositions in a letter to Pobedonostsev on the subject of *The Brothers Karamazov*:

> "For I intend this sixth book, 'A Russian Monk,' which will appear on August 31, to be the answer to this **negative**

side. And I tremble for it for this reason: will it be an adequate answer? All the more so because the *answer is not a direct one aimed at propositions which have already been stated point-by-point* (in the Grand Inquisitor or earlier), but merely an oblique one. It will be something directly [and inversely] opposite to the *Weltanschauung* which has been stated already, but again, it is presented *not point-by-point*, but, so to speak, in an *artistic picture*." (*Letters*, vol. IV, p. 109)

The characteristics of Dostoevsky's form-determining ideology hold true for all sides of his polyphonic creative work.

As a result of this ideological approach it is not a world of objects, illuminated and ordered by his monological thinking, that unrolls before Dostoevsky, but a world of mutually illuminating consciousnesses, a world of coupled human philosophical orientations. He searches among them for the highest, most authoritative orientation, and he thinks of it not as his own true thought, but as another true person and his word. The image of the ideal, man or the image of Christ represents for him the solution of ideological quests. This image or this highest of voices must crown the world of voices, organize it and subdue it. Precisely the image of a man and his voice (a voice not the author's own) was the ultimate ideological criterion for Dostoevsky: not faithfulness to his own convictions, and not the merit of the convictions themselves, taken abstractly, but precisely faithfulness to the authoritative image of the man.[81]

In answer to Kavelin, Dostoevsky jotted in his notebook:

> "It is not enough to define morality as faithfulness to one's convictions. One must constantly ask oneself: are my convictions just? There is only one test for them—Christ. This is no longer philosophy, but faith, and faith is a red light ...
>
> I cannot call a burner of heretics a moral man, because I do not recognize your thesis that morality is agreement with inner convictions. That is only **honesty** (Russian is a rich language), not morality. I have a moral model and ideal—Christ. I ask—would he have burned heretics?—no. That means that the burning of heretics is an immoral act ...

Christ was mistaken—it's been proved! A burning feeling tells me: better to remain with a mistake, with Christ, than with you ...

Living life has flown away from you, and only formulas and categories are left, but that seems to make you happy. That way one has more peace and quiet, you say (laziness) ...

You say that only acting according to convictions is moral. But where did they come from? I simply do not believe you, and I say, on the contrary, it is immoral to act according to convictions. And of course you cannot prove me wrong."[82]

The important thing in these thoughts is not Dostoevsky's Christian confession of faith in and of itself, but the living forms of his artistic and ideological thinking which are here recognized and clearly expressed. Formulas and categories are foreign to his thinking. He prefers to err, but remain with Christ, i.e. to be without truth in the theoretical sense, without truth-as-formula or truth-as-proposition. His *putting a question* (What would Christ do?) to his ideal image is extremely characteristic; it illustrates his inner dialogical orientation to the image; he does not merge with it, but follows in its path.

Characteristic of Dostoevsky's form-determining ideology are the following: distrust of convictions and their usual monological function; the quest for truth not as a conclusion of one's consciousness, but rather in the ideal, authoritative image of another person; an orientation toward the voice and word of another person. The author's idea or thought must not have the function of totally illuminating the world represented in the work; it must take its place in the work as the image of a person, an orientation among other orientations, a word among other words. This ideal orientation (the true word) must be kept in view, but it must not taint the work with the author's personal ideological tone.

In the plan for *The Life of a Great Sinner* we find the following very revealing section:

1. THE OPENING PAGES. 1) **Tone**, 2) squeeze in the thoughts artistically and concisely. The first notabene is the *Tone* (the story is a Life, i.e. although told by the author, but concisely, not skimping on explanations, but presenting it in

scenes. Harmony is needed here). *The dryness of the story should sometimes approach that of* **Gil Blas**. **As if** there were nothing special in the spectacular and dramatic sections.

But the *dominant idea* of the Life must be visible, i.e. the *whole dominant idea will not be explained in words* and will always remain a puzzle, but the reader should always be aware that this is a pious idea, and that the Life is such an important thing that I was justified to begin with the childhood years.—Also, *through the choice* of the **story's** *subject matter* and all of the facts in it, the *man of the future* will be constantly exposed to view and put on a pedestal.[83]

The "dominant idea" was indicated already in the plan of every one of Dostoevsky's novels. In his letters he often emphasized the extraordinary importance of the basic idea for him. In a letter to Strakhov he says of *The Idiot*: "Much in the novel was written hurriedly, much is too drawn out and did not turn out well, but some of it did turn out well. I do not stand behind the novel, but I do stand behind my idea."[84]

Of *The Devils* he writes to Maikov: "The *idea* has seduced me and I've fallen terribly in love with it, but if I state it, won't I emaciate the whole novel?—this is my problem!"[85] But the function of the dominant idea is a special one even in the plans of the novels. It does not extend beyond the bounds of the great dialog, and does not finalize it. It determines only the choice and distribution of the material ("through the choice of the story's subject matter"), and that material is the voices and viewpoints of other people, among which "the man of the future will be constantly put on a pedestal."[86]

We have already said that the idea functions as the ordinary monological principle of seeing and understanding the world only for the characters. Everything that could serve as direct expression or support for the idea is distributed among them. The author stands before the hero, before his unadulterated voice. In Dostoevsky there is no objective representation of milieu of manners and customs, of nature, of things, i.e. of all that which could be a support or prop for the author. The diverse world of things and the relationships of things which is a part of Dostoevsky's novel is presented from the heroes' viewpoint, in their spirit and tone. The author, as carrier of his own idea, does not come into direct contact with a single thing, only with people. It is clear that both the ideological leitmotif and the ideological conclusion, which turns its material into an object, are impossible in this world of subjects.

In 1878 Dostoevsky wrote to one of his correspondents:

> "Add to this [he had been speaking of man's non-submission to a universal law of nature—M.B.] my 'I', which perceived everything. If it perceived all of this, i.e. the whole earth and its axiom [the law of self-preservation—M.B.], then my 'I' is higher than all of this, or at least is not limited to this, but stands, as it were, off to the side, above all of this, judging and perceiving it ... In that case this 'I' not only is not subject to the earthly axiom and earthly law, it goes beyond them and has a higher law."[87]

This chiefly idealistic assessment of the consciousness was not monologically applied in Dostoevsky's artistic works. He presents the perceiving and discriminating "I" and the world as its object not in the singular, but in the plural. Dostoevsky overcame solipsism. He reserved the idealistic consciousness not for himself, but for his heroes, and not for one of them, but for all of them. In place of the relationship of the perceiving and discriminating "I" to the world, the problem of the interrelationships of these perceiving and discriminating "I's" stood at the center of his creative work.

Notes

75. The idealism of Plato is not purely monologic. It becomes purely monologic only in a neo-Kantian interpretation. Nor is Platonic dialogue of the pedagogical type, although there is a strong element of monologism in it. We shall discuss the Platonic dialogues in greater detail below, in connection with the generic traditions of Dostoevsky (see chapter 4).

76. *Zapisnye tetradi F. M. Dostoevskogo* (The Notebooks of F.M. Dostoevsky), Moscow-Leningrad, "Academia," 1935, p. 179. L.P. Grossman speaks to this point well, using Dostoevsky's own words: "The artist 'hears, has presentiments, even sees' that 'new elements, thirsting for a new word, are rising up and going forward.' Dostoevsky wrote much later: those elements must be captured and expressed." (L. P. Grossman, "Dostoevskii-khudozhnik" [Dostoevsky the Artist], in *Tvorchestvo F. M. Dostoevskogo* (Moscow: Akademiia nauk SSSR, 1959) p. 366.

[The context of Dostoevsky's note is interesting. It is on Shakespeare, and the paragraph continues: "From time to time prophets appear who divine and utter this integral word. Shakespeare was a prophet sent by God to proclaim to us the mysteries of man and the human soul."]

77. This book, published while Dostoevsky was working on *Crime and Punishment*, found great resonance in Russia. See F.I. Evnin, "Roman *Prestuplenie I nakazame*," in *Tvorchesvo F. M. Dostoevskogo*, ibid., pp. 153–57.

78. On this, see F.I. Evnin, "Roman *Besy*," ibid., pp. 228–29.

79. On this, see the book by A.S. Dolinin, *V tvorcheskoi laboratorii Dostoevskogo* [In Dostoevsky's Creative Laboratory] (Moscow, Sovetskii pisatel', 1947).

80. *PS* XI, pp. 11–15: The *Diary of a Writer*, 1873, "The Milieu," pp. 9–14.

81. We have in mind here, of course, not a finalized and closed image of reality (a type, a character, a temperament), but an open image-discourse. Such an ideal authoritative image, one not contemplated but followed, was only envisioned by Dostoevsky as the ultimate limit of his artistic project: this image was never realized in his work.

82. *Biografiia, pis'ma i zametki iz zapisnoi knizhki F.M. Dostoevskogo* [Biography, Letters and Notes from F.M. Dostoevsky's Notebook] (St. Petersburg, 1883), pp. 371–73, 374.

83. *Dokumenty po istorii literatury i obshchestvennosti*, Issue I: "F.M. Dostoevskii" (Moscow: Tsentrarkhiv RSFSR, 1922), pp. 71–72. [An English version of the plan and discussion of it can be found in Konstantin Mochulsky, *Dostoevsky: His Life and Work*, trans. Michael A. Minihan (Princeton, 1967), pp. 398–403.]

84. *Pis'ma*, II, p. 170. [Dostoevsky to N.N. Strakhov from Florence, 26 Feb./10 March, 1869.]

85. *Pis'ma*, II, p. 333. [Dostoevsky to A.N. Maikov from Dresden, 2/14 March, 1871.]

86. In a letter to Maikov Dostoevsky says: "In the second story I want to put forth as the main figure Tikhon Zadonsky, of course under another name, but he also will live peacefully in a monastery as a high-ranking member of the clergy ... Perhaps I shall make of him a majestic, *positive* holy figure. He is not a Kostanzhoglo, not the German (I've forgotten his name) in Oblomov ... and not a Lopukhov not a Rakhmetov. *To tell the truth, I won't create a thing.* I'll simply put forth the real Tikhon, whom I have long ago taken joyously into my heart." (*Pis'ma*, II, p. 264) [Dostoevsky to A.N. Maikov, from Dresden, 25 March/6 April, 1870.) A larger chunk of this letter to Maikov is translated in Mochulsky, op. cit., pp. 396–98.]

87. F.M. Dostoevskii, *Pis'ma*, IV, p. 5 [Dostoevsky to N.L. Ozmidov, February 1878.]

Chronology

1821	On October 30, Dostoevsky is born in Moscow in a hospital for the poor, he is the second of seven children.
1831–37	Fyodor and his older brother, Mikhail (b. 1820), attend boarding schools together in Moscow.
1837	On Februrary 27, Dostoevsky's mother dies; Fyodor and Mikhail are sent to a preparatory school in St. Petersburg.
1838	Dostoevsky is admitted to St. Petersburg's Academy of Military Engineers.
June 1839	Dostoevsky's father dies, possibly murdered by the serfs at his estate, Chermashnya, in the province of Tula.
1843	Doestoevsky graduates from the academy as lieutenant.
1844	Dostoevsky's translation of Balzac's *Eugenie Grandet* is published; he translates George Sand's *La derniere Aldini* and works on *Poor Folk*.
1845	Dostoevsky finishes *Poor Folk*; he is acclaimed by the influential critic, Vissarion Belinsky, and he meets Turgenyev.
1846	*Poor Folk* is published; *The Double* appears two weeks later; meets Mikhail Petrashevsky and joins his utopian Socialist study group; Anna Grigryevna Snitkina, his second wife, is born on August 30; "Mr. Prkharchin" is published in October.

1847–49	*A Novel in Nine Letters*, and "The Landlady" are published. "A Weak Heart," "An Honest Thief" and *White Nights* are published. The unfinished *Netochka Nezvanova* is published; Dostoevsky is arrested and convicted for political crimes; he is sentenced to mock execution and then to four years hard labor and an indefinite term in the army in Siberia.
1850–54	Does hard labor in Siberian prison in Omsk.
1853	Dostoevsky's epileptic seizures begin.
1854–59	Dostoevsky is released from penal servitude, begins sentence as a common soldier in Semipalatinsk near the Mongolian border.
1856	Dostoevsky is promoted to the rank of ensign.
1857	Marries Marya Dmitrievna Isaeva; the rank of nobleman is restored to him; his story, "A Little Hero," written in 1849 is published in *Notes of the Fatherland*.
1859	Dostoevsky returns to St. Petersburg. "Uncle's Dream" and "The Village of Stepanchikovo" are published.
1860	The first part of *Notes from the House of the Dead* is published. Begins to edit *Time* with his brother Mikhail; he publishes *The Insulted and the Injured* and *Memoirs from The House of the Dead* in *Time (Vremya)*. The second part of *House of the Dead* is published in *Time*. Dostoevsky travels to Europe; begins liaison with Apollinaria (Polina) Suslova.
1863–65	*Winter Notes on Summer Impressions* is published in *Time*. *Time* is ordered to cease publication by Imperial decree in April; Dostoevsky makes second trip to Europe, August–October; *Notes from Underground* is published; Dostoevsky's wife dies in April; his brother and co-editor, Mikhail, dies in July; assumes the burden of Mikhail's debts. *Epoch* ceases publication; Dostoevsky makes third trip to Europe.
1866–68	*Crime and Punishment* and *The Gambler* are published. Dostoevsky marries Anna Grigoryevna Snitkina; they leave for Western Europe, and remain abroad for four

	years. His daughter Sonya is born in February and dies three months later; Dostoevsky publishes *The Idiot* serially in *Russian Messenger.*
1869	Doestoevsky's daughter Lyubov is born in September.
1870	Publishes *The Eternal Husband* in *Dawn.*
1871–72	Returns to St. Petersburg; *The Devils* is published serially in *Russian Messenger*.
1873	Dostoevsky becomes editor of the conservative journal *The Citizen;* he begins "Diary of a Writer" as a column in *The Citizen.*
1874	Dostoevsky is imprisoned for two days for violation of censorship regulations; Anna begins their own publishing company and publishes *The Devils*; *The Idiot* is published in book form; Dostoevsky takes first of four trips to Bad Ems, a health spa in Germany, for treatment of emphysema.
1875	Publishes *A Raw Youth* in *Notes of the Fatherland*; Son, Alyosha is born; dies three years later.
1876	Dostoevsky founds *The Diary of a Writer* as a journal with himself as the only contributor; he publishes *A Gentle Creature* in it.
1877	Publishes *The Dream of a Ridiculous Man.*
1879–80	*The Brothers Karamazov* is published serially in *Russian Messenger*; Anna opens a direct-mail book service. Dostoevsky delivers speech on Pushkin at the Pushkin festivities in Moscow in June 1880.
1881	Dostoevsky dies from a lung hemorrhage in St. Petersburg on January 28 at the age of 59. He is buried February 1 in the cemetery of Alexander Nevsky Monastery.

Works by Fyodor Dostoevsky

Eugénie Grandet (Honoré de Balzac), 1844 [translation].

Poor Folk, 1846.

The Double, 1846.

"Mr. Prokharchin," 1846.

"A Novel in Nine Letters," 1847.

"The Landlady," 1847.

"Another Man's Wife; or, The Husband Under the Bed," 1848.

"A Faint Heart," 1848.

"Polzunkov," 1848.

"Out of the Service," 1848.

"An Honest Thief," 1848.

"A Christmas Tree and a Wedding," 1848.

"White Nights," 1848.

Netochka Nezvanova, 1849.

"The Little Hero," 1857.

"Uncle's Dream," 1859.

"The Village of Stepanchikovo" ["The Friend of the Family"], 1859.

The Insulted and Injured, 1861.

Memoirs from the House of the Dead, 1862.

"A Nasty Story," 1862.

Winter Notes on Summer Impressions, 1863.

Notes from Underground, 1864.

"The Crocodile," 1865.

Crime and Punishment, 1866.

The Gambler, 1867.

The Idiot, 1868.

The Eternal Husband, 1870.

Demons [*The Possessed*], 1872.

"Bobok," 1873.

A Raw Youth [*The Adolescent*], 1875.

"The Peasant Marey," 1876.

"The Heavenly Christmas Tree," 1876.

"A Gentle Creature," 1876.

The Diary of a Writer, 1876.

"The Dream of a Ridiculous Man," 1877.

The Brothers Karamazov, 1880.

"The Pushkin Address," 1880.

* * * *

Excellent versions in English of the major novels have been translated by the husband-and-wife team of Richard Pevear and Larissa Volokhonsky.

Works about Fyodor Dostoevsky

Anderson, Nancy K. *The Perverted Ideal in Dostoevsky's* The Devils. New York: Peter Lang, 1997.

Bakhtin, Mikhail. *Problems of Dostoevsky's Poetics*. Trans. R.W. Rotsel. Ann Arbor: Ardis, 1973.

Belknap, Robert L. "The Rhetoric of an Ideological Novel." *Literature and Society in Imperial Russia, 1800–1914*, ed. William Mills Todd III, 197–223. Stanford: Stanford University Press, 1978.

———. *The Structure of* The Brothers Karamazov. The Hague: Mouton, 1967.

Berdyaev, Nicholas. *Dostoevsky*. Trans. Donald Attwater. New York: Meridien, 1960.

Braun, Maximilian. "*The Brothers Karamazov* as an Expository Novel." *Canadian-American Slavic Studies* 6.2 (1972): 199–208.

Busch, R. L. *Humor in the Major Novels of F.M. Dostoevsky*. Columbus: Slavica, 1987.

Catteau, Jacques. *Dostoyevsky and the Process of Literary Creation*. Trans. Audrey Littlewood. Cambridge: Cambridge University Press, 1989.

Cerny, Vaclav. *Dostoevsky and His Devils*. Trans. F.W. Galan. Ann Arbor: Ardis, 1975.

Cox, Gary. *Tyrant and Victim in Dostoevsky*. Columbus: Slavica, 1983.

Dalton, Elizabeth. *Unconscious Structure in* The Idiot: *A Study in Literature and Psychoanalysis*. Princeton: Princeton University Press, 1979.

Davidson, R.M. *"The Devils*: The Role of Stavrogin." *New Essays on Dostoyevsky*, eds. Malcolm V. Jones and Garth M. Terry, 95–114. Cambridge: Cambridge University Press, 1983.

Dostoevsky, Fyodor. *The Notebooks for* The Idiot. Ed. Edward Wasiolek. Chicago: University of Chicago Press, 1967.

Fanger, Donald. *Dostoevsky and Romantic Realism: A Study of Dostoevsky in Relation to Balzac, Dickens, and Gogol*. Cambridge: Harvard University Press, 1965.

Frank, Joseph. *Dostoevsky: The Mantle of the Prophet, 1871–1881*. Princeton: Princeton University Press, 2002.

———. *Dostoevsky: The Miraculous Years, 1865–1871*. Princeton: Princeton University Press, 1995.

Girard, René. *Deceit, Desire, and the Novel: Self and Other in Literary Structure*. Trans. Yvonne Freccero. Baltimore: Johns Hopkins Press, 1965.

Guardini, Romano. "Dostoyevsky's Idiot, A Symbol of Christ." Trans. Francis X. Quinn. *Cross Currents* 6.4 (1956): 359–82.

Gill, Richard. "The Bridges of St. Petersburg: A Motif in *Crime and Punishment*." *Dostoevsky Studies* 3 (1982): 145–55.

Guerard, Albert J. "On the Composition of Dostoevsky's *The Idiot*." *Mosaic* 8.1 (1974): 200–15.

Holquist, Michael. *Dostoevsky and the Novel*. Princeton: Princeton University Press, 1977.

Ivanov, Vyacheslav. *Freedom and the Tragic Life: A Study in Dostoevsky*. Trans. Norman Cameron. London: Harvill Press, 1952.

Jones, John. *Dostoevsky*. Oxford: Clarendon Press, 1983.

Kurrick, Maire Jaanus. *Literature and Negation*. New York: Columbia University Press, 1979.

Leatherbarrow, W.J., ed. *Dostoevsky's* The Devils: A Critical Companion. Evanston: Northwestern University Press, 1999.

Matlaw, Ralph E. "The Chronicler of *The Possessed*: Character and Function." *Dostoevsky Studies* 5 (1984): 37–47.

Matlaw, Ralph E. "Recurrent Imagery in Dostoevskij." *Harvard Slavic Studies* 3 (1957): 201–25.

Meijer, J.M. "Situation Rhyme in a Novel of Dostoevskij." *Dutch Contributions to the Fourth International Congress of Slavicists, Moscow, September 1958*, 115–29. The Hague: Mouton, 1958.

Miller, Robin Feuer. "The Role of the Reader in *The Idiot*." *Slavic and East European Journal* 23.2 (1979): 190–202.

Mochulsky, Konstantin. *Dostoevsky: His Life and Work*. Trans. Michael A. Minihan. Princeton: Princeton University Press, 1967.

Morson, Gary Saul. "Verbal Pollution in *The Brothers Karamazov*." *PTL: A Journal for Descriptive Poetics and Theory of Literature* 3 (1978): 25–44.

Nuttall, A.D. Crime and Punishment: *Murder as Philosophic Experiment*. Edinburgh: Sussex University Press, 1978.

Passage, Charles E. *Character Names in Dostoevsky's Fiction*. Ann Arbor: Ardis, 1982.

Peace, Richard. *Dostoyevsky: An Examination of the Major Novels*. Cambridge: Cambridge University Press, 1971.

Proffer, Carl R. *The Unpublished Dostoevsky: Diaries and Notebooks (1860–81)*. 3 vols. Trans. T. S. Berczynski, Barbara Heldt Monter, Arline Boyer, and Ellendea Proffer. Ann Arbor: Ardis, 1973.

Rahv, Philip. *Essays on Literature and Politics, 1932–1972*. Eds. Arabel J. Porter and Andrew J. Dvosin. Boston: Houghton Mifflin, 1978.

Rosen, Nathan. "Style and Structure in *The Brothers Karamazov*: The Grand Inquisitor and the Russian Monk." *Russian Literature Triquarterly* 1 (1971): 352–65.

———. "Why Dmitrii Karamazov Did Not Kill His Father." *Canadian-American Slavic Studies* 6.2 (1972): 209–24.

Rosenshield, Gary. Crime and Punishment: *The Techniques of the Omniscient Author*. Lisse: Peter de Ridder, 1978.

Sandoz, Ellis. *Political Apocalypse: A Study of Dostoevsky's Grand Inquisitor*. Baton Rouge: Louisiana State University Press, 1971.

Seduro, Vladimir. *Dostoyevsky in Russian Literary Criticism 1846–1956*. New York: Columbia University Press, 1957.

Simmons, Ernest J. *Dostoevsky: The Making of a Novelist*. London: John Lehmann, 1950.

Terras, Victor. *A Karamazov Companion*. Madison: University of Wisconsin Press, 1981.

Vivas, Eliseo. "The Two Dimensions of Reality in *The Brothers Karamazov*." *Sewanee Review* 59 (1951): 23–49.

Wasiolek, Edward, ed. Crime and Punishment *and the Critics*. San Francisco: Wadsworth, 1961.

Wasiolek, Edward. *Dostoevsky: The Major Fiction*. Cambridge: MIT Press, 1964.

Welch, Lois M. "Luzhin's Crime and the Advantages of Melodrama in Dostoevsky's *Crime and Punishment*." *Texas Studies in Literature and Language* 18 (1976): 135–46.

Wellek, René. *Dostoevsky: A Collection of Critical Essays*. Englewood Cliffs: Prentice-Hall, 1962.

Wharton, Robert V. "Dostoevsky's Defense of Christ in *The Brothers Karamazov*: Part Two." *Cithara* 24.1 (1984): 59–70.

———. "Roads to Happiness in *The Brothers Karamazov*: Dostoevsky's Defense of Christ." *Cithara* 23.2 (1984): 3–15.

WEBSITES

Fyodor Dostoevsky—The Literature Network
http://www.online-literature.com/dostoevsky/

Fyodor Dostoevsky
http://www.kirjasto.sci.fi/fdosto.htm

Bibliomania—Fyodor Dostoevsky
http://www.bibliomania.com/0/0/235/frameset.html

Wikipedia—Fyodor Dostoevsky
http://en.wikipedia.org/wiki/Fyodor_Dostoevsky

Contributors

HAROLD BLOOM is Sterling Professor of the Humanities at Yale University. He is the author of over 20 books, including *Shelley's Mythmaking* (1959), *The Visionary Company* (1961), *Blake's Apocalypse* (1963), *Yeats* (1970), *A Map of Misreading* (1975), *Kabbalah and Criticism* (1975), *Agon: Toward a Theory of Revisionism* (1982), *The American Religion* (1992), *The Western Canon* (1994), and *Omens of Millennium: The Gnosis of Angels, Dreams, and Resurrection* (1996). *The Anxiety of Influence* (1973) sets forth Professor Bloom's provocative theory of the literary relationships between the great writers and their predecessors. His most recent books include *Shakespeare: The Invention of the Human* (1998), a 1998 National Book Award finalist, *How to Read and Why* (2000), *Genius: A Mosaic of One Hundred Exemplary Creative Minds* (2002), and *Hamlet: Poem Unlimited* (2003). In 1999, Professor Bloom received the prestigious American Academy of Arts and Letters Gold Medal for Criticism, and in 2002 he received the Catalonia International Prize.

NEIL HEIMS is a freelance writer, editor, and researcher. He has a Ph.D. in English from the City University of New York. Neil has worked on Albert Camus and J.R.R. Tolkien volumes for Chelsea House.

RACHEL THOMAS is a freelance author who earned her B.A. in Humanities from Yale University. Her thesis, on concepts of Christianity in the works of William Blake, was written under the guidance of Harold Bloom. This is her second contribution to the *Bloom Biocritiques* series, following an essay on Maya Angelou. Thomas works full-time as Program Coordinator for the Yale Women Faculty Forum.

WILLIAM MILLS TODD III is Harry Tuchman Levin Professor of Literature and Professor of Comparative Literature at Harvard University. His works include *Fiction and Society in the Age of Pushkin: Ideology, Institutions, Narrative* and *Soviet Sociology of Literature: Conceptions of a Changing World*.

VICTOR TERRAS is Professor Emeritus of Slavic Languages at Brown University. He has written *A History of Russian Literature* and is the editor of the *Handbook of Russian Literature*.

MIKHAIL BAKHTIN (1895–1975) was a leading Soviet critic and literary theorist. He wrote numerous essays and books, such as *Art & Answerability: Early Philosophical Essays* and *The Dialogic Imagination: Four Essays*.

INDEX